JUST BUSINESS

Visit us at www.boldstrokesbooks.com

Praise for Julie Cannon

Heart 2 Heart

"*Heart 2 Heart* has many hot, intense sex scenes; Lane and Kyle sizzle across the pages…Cannon has given her readers a read that's fun as well as meaty." — *JustAboutWrite*

Heartland

"…There's nothing coy about the passion of these unalike dykes—it ignites at first encounter, and never abates… Cannon's well-constructed novel conveys more complexity of character and less overwrought melodrama than most stories in the crowded genre of lesbian-love-against-all-odds—a definite plus." — *Book Marks*

"Julie Cannon has created a wonderful romance. Rachel and Shivley are believable, likeable, bright, and funny. The scenery of the ranch is beautifully described, down to the smells, work, and dust. This is an extremely engaging book, full of humor, drama, and some very hot, hot sex!" — *JustAboutWrite*

By the Author

Come and Get Me

Heart 2 Heart

Heartland

Uncharted Passage

JUST BUSINESS

by
Julie Cannon

2009

JUST BUSINESS

© 2009 By Julie Cannon. All Rights Reserved.

ISBN 10: 1-60282-052-X
ISBN 13: 978-1-60282-052-4

This Trade Paperback Original Is Published By
Bold Strokes Books, Inc.
P.O. Box 249
Valley Falls, NY 12185

First Edition: March 2009

Credits

Editors: Shelley Thrasher and Stacia Seaman
Production Design: Stacia Seaman
Cover Design By Sheri (graphicartist2020@hotmail.com)

Acknowledgments

My thanks go out to all the women at BSB who work in front of and behind the pages. Without you, all of this would not be possible. My special thanks to Shelley Thrasher, who was great to work with, and Sheri, whose cover took my breath away (again).

Dedication

For my family

PROLOGUE

I now pronounce you married in the eyes of the Lord, your friends, and family. You may kiss the bride."

Dillon turned from the elderly gentleman wearing a white collar to the woman in the pale blue dress who stood beside her. Callie Sheffield was arguably the most beautiful woman Dillon had ever seen. Crystal-clear blue eyes looked at her expectantly. A shy smile she had come to know over these past few months held her attention, while a warm hand cupped her face.

"You're supposed to kiss me now."

The voice was soft and melodious, teasing in its inflection. Callie—insightful, intuitive, and always right—was one of the few people Dillon Matthews allowed to actually tell her what to do. She knew how to listen to those around her, especially when they knew more about something than she did.

She bent her head and kissed the red lips as instructed, and a wave of heat practically welded her feet to the floor. The taste of Callie's lips made her forget where she was and how long she stood there.

Finally, she released them and faced the crowd of people who sat in the church's hard-backed pews. Some were friends, others were business associates, and dozens were people she had never seen before.

She took a deep, shaky breath. By all accounts this should have been the happiest day of her life, but as she gazed at the sixty faces that stared back at her, all she could think was, "How in the hell did I get here?"

Chapter One

H e what?" Dillon Matthews was dumbfounded.
"You heard me. He's not sure he wants you to have his
property. Bill Franklin is a crotchety old man, Dillon. It's his land,
and he can sell it to whomever he wants for whatever reason."

"Does he know who I am? How much money I'm offering
him? For God's sake. I'm one of the richest women in America. His
land holdings are nothing, compared to mine."

"Yes, he does, and that's why he's digging in his heels. Price
isn't the sticking point."

"Then what is? I'm offering more than three times what that
land is worth, which is more than anyone else will give him for it."
Dillon paced the large conference room located on the fiftieth floor
of the Matthews Building. The plush carpet muffled her footsteps,
and the triple-pane glass kept the cold spring day outside.

She turned her back on the ragged skyline of Chicago and
walked across her spacious office to the three-dimensional scale
replica of her largest land-development project yet. Gateway was
to be built on twelve acres of lakefront property running parallel to
Lake Michigan along Lake Shore Drive. It consisted of four hundred
thousand feet of retail and office space, flanked by two high-end
residential towers.

"Greg, I need this parcel of land. Bill Franklin is the last thing
standing between me and Gateway. I can't build without his measly
four acres. Well, I can, but a much smaller version that will end up

looking choppy and like every other commercial-use property in the country. We have a reputation to maintain, and boring buildings are not part of it."

Properties designed and built by Matthews Holdings were anything but conventional and boring. They were splashes of color projected over aggressive designs that mirrored their architect/ owner. Dillon's thumbprint was easily recognizable around the world. The bold, daring design of her buildings usually stretched the bounds of engineering capability with a mixture of glass, steel, light, shadow, and texture, all intricately woven together in a well-choreographed dance. Often her designs formed the cornerstone of major redevelopment projects, and recently she not only owned the buildings she designed but the land on which they stood. Nothing stood in the way of her creativity or her desire to make a name for herself in the land-development community. Nothing until seventy-eight-year-old Bill Franklin blocked her path.

"He's invited you to his house for dinner two weeks from Saturday."

"Dinner? This is a business deal, not a social event."

In the early years of her career, Dillon was the deal maker, the one who set the terms, negotiated every detail. Now she had people to take care of that chore. As a matter of fact, she had people to take care of almost everything. She rarely became involved in the negotiations other than to sign the contract and the check.

She shook her head at the idiosyncrasies of an old man. "All right, I'll do whatever it takes to convince him to sell to me."

Dillon had to have this property. Gateway would be the culmination of everything she had dreamed of. And she had worked hard to get it. After putting herself through college, she had traveled to France and graduated at the top of her class from Le Solamonde, the world's most prestigious architectural school. She could have worked at any firm she chose, but she decided to venture out on her own, knowing that any boss other than herself would squelch her style and creativity.

In the past ten years she had made a name for herself, and the architectural community anticipated Gateway. But most important, she expected herself to stun everyone. She needed this project to make her father finally look at her with something other than disappointment.

"Oh, and Dillon." Greg hesitated.

Dillon was already moving on to the pile of papers on her desk but looked up at the pause.

"It *is* a social call. Bring a date."

Dillon cocked her head. "I don't *date*." She was perplexed by Greg's last statement. He knew very well that she preferred the women in her life to be gorgeous and temporary.

"Then you'd better hire someone. Franklin is expecting you and a date at his house for dinner. This is *not* a business meeting, Dillon. I get the impression that a healthy balance between work and life is important to him. I think he wants to see that there's more to you than your business persona."

Dillon dropped the folder she was examining onto her desk. "Oh, for God's sake, Greg. It's a piece of land, not my ticket to heaven. The only thing he should care about is how fast my check clears the bank."

"That's the way you and I think, Dillon. Evidently that's not how Franklin sees things."

"Does he know I'm a lesbian? I'll do a lot of things for a deal, but pretending I'm straight isn't one of them. I'm way past that crap."

In the early years of Dillon's career she had not openly discussed the fact that she was a lesbian, preferring to attend social functions alone rather than draw attention to herself by taking a woman as her date. She wasn't hiding anything. She simply didn't want to be judged by who she brought with her. At least she didn't try to pretend to be someone she wasn't by arriving with a man. But this evening was different. She had practically been told to invite someone, and she didn't like being told what to do. As important as this dinner was with Franklin, she was just maverick enough to choose who *she* wanted.

"As a matter of fact, he said something about looking forward to being surrounded by intelligent, beautiful women at the dinner table." Dillon slumped back in her chair. "Look, Dillon, for some reason he considers this more than just a business deal. If you want this piece of land, you'd better show up with June Cleaver on your arm."

Greg closed the door behind him, leaving Dillon alone. The image of the 1960s television sitcom *Leave it to Beaver* flashed into her mind. Interestingly, she had stumbled across the old show last week on a business trip while flipping through the channels on the hotel television in search of CNN. June Cleaver was every man's dream of a wife—always perfectly coiffed, performing her domestic duties in high heels and a dress. Dillon wondered if June wore her pearls when she performed her other wifely duties.

Shaking that image away, Dillon reached for her Rolodex, but stopped. She knew dozens of women more than willing to accompany her for the evening. The women she went out with were poised, smart, sophisticated, and refined. In other words, everything she needed for an audition dinner with Franklin, but for some reason none of them felt right.

Her phone rang, drawing her attention back to the pile of work on her desk. She finished the call in minutes and spun her chair around to face the window, lifting her feet to the top of the credenza that ran the length of the desk behind her. This was her favorite position—hands locked behind her head, gazing at the sky as if it were her canvas to sculpt and create. Each season provided different inspiration, the changing weather guiding her pencil strokes on the thick pad she always kept nearby. Summer brought blue sky and an openness to her designs that often captured the essence of light. Winter, with its drab days and cold, bitter wind, transformed itself into structures full of oversized columns, archways, and deep corridors. Days like today, early spring with just enough chill in the air to remind her that winter was not yet ready to give up but enough warmth to give her hope, often gave birth to her most creative, cutting-edge designs. Gateway was born two years ago in the very position she was in now.

She shifted her gaze to the ground below, watching the people in the city carry on their everyday lives fifty stories below. They probably passed the same familiar faces on the street every day but never stopped to say hello or exchange anything other than a polite, cursory greeting.

Dillon could relate—she worked hard, played hard, but, with the exception of her sister, she didn't really connect to people. Early on in her career she often wondered if something was wrong with her, if she was missing the connection gene, the DNA that drove people to link up with others. She wasn't a social person, didn't need to be around people, but preferred to concentrate on her work. At times she felt more related to her buildings, structures, and designs than to humanity.

However, Greg was an exception. He was more than her assistant. He was her friend, and they usually had dinner together a couple of times a month. She could easily count her other friends on the same hand with a finger or two missing. Her sister Laura probably knew her best, her parents often distant and aloof.

Dillon shook her head as she pictured her father's face years ago when she told him she wanted to be an architect and not crawl up the corporate ladder as he had at Chicago's most conservative law firm. She didn't know which he considered worse—coming out of the closet or not wanting her name in gold-embossed letters on the front door. He had never looked at her the same, and Dillon had never looked back.

Swinging her feet to the floor, she turned her attention to the current task, however distasteful. *A date?* She began to outline her plan of attack to find Ms. Right. Certainly within two weeks she could find the perfect woman, couldn't she?

CHAPTER TWO

Callie Sheffield nursed her second beer as the music that surrounded her pulsed with the incessant beat of a scratched record. The same three notes played over and over and over as the sound pounded into her brain. No wonder nonstop loud music was used as a form of torture and brainwashing. She would do almost anything to get it to stop.

The door of the Incognito Lounge opened again and she glanced at it, hoping Audrey had finally arrived. She had been waiting for her best friend for over an hour, and if she didn't show in the next ten minutes, she was leaving. She had agreed to meet Audrey here at nine thirty, knowing from long experience that she was habitually late.

Callie was beginning to simmer. She had already repelled several women who obviously thought she was an easy pickup because she was sitting alone at the end of the bar. Ten or fifteen years ago she probably was, but at thirty-six, Callie had more important things in her life than meaningless, if sexually satisfying, one-night stands. But then the Incognito was known as a pickup bar both in reputation and ambience.

Twenty-odd years ago when it opened, the Incog, as the regulars called it, was *the* place to be. The newest women's club in town, it boasted the latest sound system, the hottest disc jockeys, and the stiffest drinks. Now, almost two decades older and several owners later, it had fallen into being just another tired lesbian bar with worn carpet and a bar chipped and stained from one too many sweating glasses and forgotten cigarettes. The twelve-inch-square mirrors that covered the walls reflected little more than the twinkling, long-forgotten Christmas lights that hung from the ceiling. Even though Chicago had enacted a no-smoking ordinance in bars several years earlier, the smell of stale cigarettes had permeated every fixture, beam, and pool table.

Callie's thoughts shifted to the one subject that had consumed her for the past three years: Michael. Every time she thought of her baby brother, she envisioned a small boy with black hair sticking out in all directions riding his skateboard up and down the driveway of their home. That little boy had grown into a tall, handsome man with a constant smile and a great sense of humor. Even though she was ten years older, Michael always looked after her. He told her it was his responsibility as her brother to take care of her regardless of their reverse birth order.

Callie swallowed a mouthful of now-warm beer, trying to dislodge the familiar lump in her throat. When she saw Michael last week, a flat, hollow look had replaced the sparkle in his eyes. She wanted to gather him in her arms and hold him until that light returned. But she couldn't. It would be thirty-five years, ten months, and twenty-two days until she could touch him again. Her little brother would be over sixty years old when he was released from Lompak Maximum Correctional Facility for killing the man who had beaten and tried to rape her.

The beat of the music assaulted Dillon as soon as she stepped out of her car. She could barely hear the chirping of the car alarm above the bass, and she had to turn around to see the lights blink on her BMW to convince herself the car was secure. One of her cars had been stolen from this parking lot, and she didn't want it to happen again. The money didn't bother her. She had more than enough to cover what the insurance didn't. The paperwork was the pain in the ass. She slipped a fifty to the security guard and thanked him for letting her park in one of the coveted places near the front of the building. When she opened the door, the decibels of the music almost knocked her down.

Nodding to the bouncer and paying the ten-dollar cover charge, Dillon practically fell over a couple locked in an embrace that, if done anywhere other than inside a lesbian bar, would be cause for arrest. She looked again and revised her opinion. They very easily could be arrested for what they were doing. The tingle of arousal that accompanied the scene reminded her that she hadn't had sex in far too long, and a sweeping glance around the room told her she could most probably rectify that problem soon.

She weaved through the throng of women and signaled to the bartender for her usual drink. Dillon had frequented this bar since before she was legally old enough. While on a high-school class trip to Mexico, she and her friends bought fake IDs that added four years to their age, granting them access to any bar in the city. The Incognito was the first lesbian bar she had ever entered, and she would always remember the way she felt when she walked in. The sight of women dancing together, kissing each other, holding hands, and laughing was the most affirming she had ever seen. No matter how young the crowd or how old the posters on the wall, the Incog would always be special to her.

As she exchanged a five-dollar bill for a bottle of Fat Tire, she saw just over the left shoulder of the bartender a woman sitting alone, peeling the label off her own beer bottle. Ordinarily Dillon wouldn't have even noticed her, experience telling her that someone like her usually sat alone at the bar for a reason, and she always stayed clear. But something was different about this one, and after Dillon squeezed past the other patrons who had crowded behind her for their turn at the bar, she moved so she could see her more clearly.

Propping herself against the wall, Dillon drank her beer, watching the woman do the same. After a few minutes she traded her empty bottle for a full one, subtly appraising the woman as if she were judging her for some type of contest. Nothing about her was special. Even from across the room Dillon suspected her short, wavy blond hair was soft and thick. The sleeves of her royal blue shirt were rolled up to her elbows, and Dillon liked the casual, unpretentious way she had dispensed of them, unlike the perfectly folded cuffs of the woman sitting two stools to her left. The blonde's arms were tan, revealing hands free of any rings. Her glasses were stylish, perched on top of a slightly crooked nose, and the small hoops hanging from her ears were the kind worn by half the women in the room. The only other visible jewelry Dillon saw was a clunky watch that the woman kept glancing at every few minutes. She was either waiting for someone or deciding whether to go home.

A pang grabbed Dillon's stomach when a stunning brunette approached the woman. Dillon knew by the intruder's body language that she was on the prowl for something other than conversation and watched in interest as she was politely but firmly rebuffed. Dillon was relieved but wasn't sure why.

An overweight dyke bumped Dillon, drawing her attention away from the woman and back to the main reason she was here. She scanned the crowd that had grown in size in the last fifteen minutes, providing her a wide variety from which to choose. The redhead she noticed when she first came in looked particularly interesting, as did the Angelina Jolie look-alike shooting pool. She nodded to a woman she had been with several times who definitely knew what to do with her mouth other than argue a case before the state supreme court. The model-thin brunette in the corner, Dillon knew firsthand, was just the opposite. But her glance kept straying back to the woman at the bar, and when Dillon looked this time, she was paying her tab, apparently about to leave. Before Dillon realized what she was doing, she had crossed the bar and stood beside her.

Callie felt rather than saw the woman and her anger rose to the surface. She was pissed at Audrey for standing her up and making her endure the bar leeches that saw her only as fresh meat. She was tired and her small headache from earlier in the day was competing with the music for space in her head. She was gathering her keys when a voice from behind her asked, "Would you like to dance?"

For an instant Callie was tempted to spit back a caustic reply, but then she realized this woman had asked her to dance, not tossed out a weak, overused pickup line. When she gave the woman her attention, Callie saw that she had not invaded her personal space like the others, had not set her beer on the bar like she had been invited, and was looking at her face, not her chest. This woman and her approach were different.

"Excuse me?" She practically had to shout to be heard over the noise.

The woman standing next to her lowered her head slightly, but didn't take advantage of the opportunity to step closer. "I asked if you would like to dance."

Callie wanted to say no, she knew she should say no, but something about the way this woman presented herself made her say yes instead. She had been acting strange lately, and this was another indication that she really needed to get it together before she did something stupid. Not until she rose off the stool did the woman put her beer on the bar. The woman signaled for her to lead the way to the dance floor, and Callie managed to find a small unoccupied space where they could barely move among the throngs of women jostling for a piece of wood-laminate real estate.

They hadn't danced more than a dozen steps when the lights dimmed and a slow ballad instantly replaced the blaring music. The woman didn't act like she wanted to leave the crowded floor but looked at Callie as if to say, "It's up to you."

Against her better judgment Callie held out her arms and the woman stepped forward. "My name is Dillon."

Callie had to tilt her head up to meet the eyes of the woman who held her chastely. She was only an inch or two taller than her own five foot six inches, but she seemed taller. "Callie."

"Pleased to meet you, Callie."

Dillon didn't say anything more, and Callie tentatively enjoyed the feeling of being held in her arms. They fit perfectly and danced well together, without the usual awkward stumbling of strangers on the dance floor.

She glanced up and met a strong chin and a firm jawline. Soft curls fell over Dillon's forehead, and only a hint of lines around her eyes indicated her age. Dillon smiled, and for the first time Callie noticed deep dimples on either side of full lips, making her look like a little girl. But the hard body so near hers was definitely that of a full-grown woman. A flush of heat scorched through her body at the thought, and she stumbled. Dillon pulled her closer, steadying her.

"Sorry," Callie replied, shaking her head to regain her equilibrium. Her hands were sweaty and she wasn't sure her legs would hold her upright. Dillon seemed to sense her insecurity and held her a little tighter. *It's the beers*, Callie thought. *They're making me light-headed.* She hadn't eaten dinner and had downed three beers. Dillon smiled and Callie stumbled again.

"It's okay. It's kind of tough dancing with someone you just met. Maybe we should do it more often, and if we get good enough we can try out for *Dancing with the Stars*."

Callie laughed at Dillon's reference to the popular television show. "But on that show the regular people dance with the stars, not with each other." Callie started to relax again.

"Do you mean to tell me you're not somebody famous? I thought you were Leann Rimes." Dillon leaned back, looking at Callie's face, their lower bodies touching intimately.

"Very funny. Leann Rimes is a country singer, not a lesbian." The pressure of Dillon's pelvis against hers was making her crotch tingle.

Dillon feigned disappointment, then smiled again. "A girl can fantasize, can't she?"

Callie's stomach fell at the expression in Dillon's eyes, which was a combination of lust, humor, and challenge. It made Callie want something she hadn't had in a long time—to get lost in those eyes. To feel soft hands stroke and caress her body, strong arms hold her after she came. She wanted to stop thinking and disappear in sensation.

She tried to force her thoughts back to reality, but that was almost impossible with this beautiful woman wrapped around her. The lights came up as quickly as they had gone down, and the shriek of an electric guitar pierced the stillness of the dance floor.

Dillon winced at the abrupt transition and made a note to talk to Joanne, the owner, about the DJ's order of songs. Reluctantly she released Callie and followed her back to where they had left their beers on the bar.

"Thank you for the dance. You're very good." Dillon almost choked on her words as Callie tilted her head back, exposing her long neck as she drank the remaining liquid in her bottle. Dillon's pulse raced and her crotch throbbed. She almost dropped her bottle when Callie laughed.

"Are you kidding? I stepped on your feet and practically fell on my ass, not once but twice. I don't know who you've been dancing with, but she certainly had to be..." Callie lost her train of thought at the barely contained look of desire burning in Dillon's eyes. She couldn't pull her own eyes away and was drawn in to the fiery depths. Dillon blinked a few times and the blaze disappeared. Had Callie imagined it? The way her body reacted told her it had been there.

"My niece," Dillon replied.

"What?" Callie asked, confused.

"My niece. The person I've been dancing with. She's six years old, and every time we get together she insists on dancing with me. She's all legs, with two left feet and a smile the size of Texas."

"She must take after her aunt," Callie replied. At the shocked look on Dillon's face she added, "The smile part. Not the two left feet." She thought for a moment then looked at Dillon's legs from the tip of her boots to the top of her thighs. "Okay, the leg part too."

Dillon flushed under Callie's direct appraisal and said, "Would you like to go somewhere a little quieter? Maybe get a cup of coffee or something?"

Callie's breath caught in her throat. "Or something?" Callie wasn't in the mood for innuendo and idle chitchat.

Dillon's eyes dilated with obvious excitement. "Yes."

"And what form of something did you have in mind?" Callie was typically not this forward with women, but she could barely remember the last time she was with one.

"I'd prefer to spell it out where there aren't so many people around. I'll tell you exactly what I have in mind if you tell me first."

Callie closed the gap between them. Her heart was pounding and her breathing was shallow. "All right. There's no need to beat around the bush. We're two consenting adults who obviously find each other attractive. Why not act on it?" Callie took a deep breath. "I want to fuck you senseless and I'd expect the same."

Chapter Three

Dillon's nagging sensation of unease intensified. Her inner voice was always correct, and it was telling her that something about Callie wasn't quite right. The hesitation in Callie's voice, which Dillon detected in spite of the blare from the speakers, made her suspect Callie wasn't used to going home with someone she had just met in a bar. When she offered exactly what Dillon had in mind, she hadn't known whether to rejoice or run.

She had been burned in the past by women who agreed to an unencumbered romp in the sack, but immediately became clingy and demanding not long after she left their bed. Callie wasn't giving off those signals, but Dillon couldn't determine what she was exuding. So she said, "I was thinking more along the lines of a cup of coffee somewhere."

The look on Callie's face told Dillon that was definitely not the response she expected.

Dillon spoke quickly. "Let me rephrase that. I'm flattered, and I will admit that was my intent when I came over here, but as tempting as it sounds, I get the impression you aren't completely comfortable with this situation. I don't want to take advantage of it, and I certainly don't want to take advantage of you."

Callie wondered why Dillon was saying these things. Was she being honest, or was she playing some kind of weird game? Maybe she shouldn't have anything to do with someone who gave such mixed signals.

"Please don't be embarrassed," Dillon said. "Any other time or place and we wouldn't make it out of the parking lot. Let's go get some coffee and we'll see where it goes from there."

Callie was mortified. At that very moment she wanted nothing more than to crawl through the seam in the tattered carpet and disappear forever. She had never been so humiliated. How could she have misjudged Dillon so badly? Granted, it had been a long time since she had allowed herself to accept a proposition for casual sex, but she didn't think she was that rusty. Dillon's signals had been clear, or at least she thought they were.

She hesitated and looked at the outstretched hand in front of her. It was a meet-in-the-middle gesture. After Dillon's rebuff, she couldn't look her in the eye. How would she be able to sit across from her in a well-lit restaurant?

"Please."

The single word was all she needed to finally decide to meet the eyes searching her face. "Do you promise to never bring this up in conversation again?" Dillon nodded. "Do you promise to never tell your friends about this?" Again, a nod. "Do you promise—"

Dillon held up her index finger. "I draw the line at promising to love, honor, and obey for as long as we both shall live. And I'm not real crazy about the better-or-worse part, either. I guess I'm selfish that way."

Callie's hesitation dissolved under Dillon's wit and dimples. "All right, but we haven't even talked about the sickness-and-health part." She was rewarded with a smile that showed off Dillon's perfectly white teeth and she accepted Dillon's hand, surprised at how comfortable it felt. As Dillon led her toward the door, she spotted Audrey leaning over a buxom blonde stretched over the pool table, stroking a pool cue and lining up her shot. A flash of irritation gave way to something else as Callie realized that if Audrey had seen her, she might not have met Dillon. She stepped out the front door into the cool night, unsure if that was a good thing or not.

❖

Dillon continued to hold Callie's hand as they walked across the busy street to the Starbucks. "This okay?" she asked as a car horn blasted behind them.

"Sure." Surprisingly, Callie didn't feel ill at ease with Dillon's firm grip as they entered the coffee shop. She wasn't one for public displays of affection, but Dillon didn't seem to want to let go. Dillon was strong and confident, and Callie needed someone to be in charge for once, even if it was only to suggest which coffee shop to go to.

She was tired—tired of making decisions, tired of fighting for every little thing. Everything seemed to be a gigantic issue that would affect the rest of her life, and lately she felt as if she had made more mistakes in judgment than correct ones. The months following the attack and Michael's arrest had passed in a blur, and she had spent the time since he had been in Lompak attending constant meetings with attorneys. Her bank balance was as dire as her decision-making ability, and neither looked like it would recover anytime soon. Thankfully her boss at the flower shop understood her occasional distraction.

She had worked at Crane Florist for six years, and the owners— Ross and his boyfriend John—had become her friends. They supported her emotionally and even continued to pay her when she had to miss work for Michael's trial and subsequent appointments. Today had been one of those days that caused her to miss lunch and dinner and drink too much at the bar.

The attorney she hired for Michael charged three hundred dollars an hour for his services, and between her brother's original defense and now his appeal, the money she had painstakingly saved to open her own flower shop was practically depleted. Ross and John didn't know it, but she had taken a second job for an answering service at night to help with the bills. This was her first night off in over three weeks. Yesterday she had started the paperwork for a second mortgage on her house, and as she filled in the information she realized that the empty boxes on the endless forms symbolized the emptiness she felt.

"Callie?"

Callie snapped her attention back to Dillon, who had an odd

look on her face. If she didn't know better, she would have thought it was a mix of concern, tenderness, and irritation. "I'm sorry. What?"

"Do you want coffee or something else?"

When Dillon had turned to Callie for her order, she looked like she was a hundred miles away. Her expression had the same almost-haunted quality that Dillon had seen earlier, and she wanted to make whatever was concerning Callie go away. She certainly had the money and power to do almost anything. Whatever was bothering Callie couldn't be that bad. Yeah. And she thought Bill Franklin would be a slam dunk too.

And what had been going on back in the bar? Dillon couldn't believe the words that had come out of her mouth. She had scruples, but when a beautiful woman offered herself, they always flew out the window. Well, almost always.

"Coffee's fine. Black, no sugar." Callie brightened and returned Dillon's gaze with a smile. Her reaction made Dillon even more curious as to what was going on with her.

Drinks in hand, Dillon led them to a round table in the corner that provided a small degree of privacy. The shop was busy, and she wanted to talk with Callie without a dozen pair of ears listening in. Callie still seemed embarrassed, so Dillon decided to keep the conversation light.

"So, what do you do when you're not out on the town?" She almost said "hanging out in a bar," but stopped herself just in time.

Callie removed her lid and blew on the hot liquid. "I work at Crane Florist."

"Doing what?"

"A little of this and a lot of that. I was hired for floral design. You know, putting all kinds of pieces together in an arrangement and making it look fabulous. But lately I've just been making deliveries and manning the cash register." Callie heard how flat and lifeless her own words sounded. And her concentration certainly wasn't what it used to be.

"What's happened lately?"

Callie sipped her coffee, giving herself a moment to decide

how to answer. Most people would have let her comment slip by, but Dillon hadn't missed her choice of words. She would have to be more careful with what she said. "I've been a little distracted. But you don't want to hear about it," she added quickly.

"Why not? Is it something gory? Better yet, is it something seedy?" Dillon leaned toward Callie.

Callie studied the woman in front of her. She had appeared out of nowhere, asked her to dance, and now here they were having coffee together. She was not going to be one of those women who dumped her life's problems on the first date. First date! Where in the hell did that come from?

"No, but I still don't want to tell you."

"Why not? I'm a good listener. Actually, I'm perfect for the part. I'm a total stranger with nothing to gain or lose by hearing your story. I'm not acquainted with any of the players, so you don't have to worry about me taking sides, and I don't know you, so I can't be judgmental. It's kind of like anonymous sex. We'll never see each other again, so why not let it all hang out?"

Callie was puzzled. She put the lid back on her coffee, not wanting it to cool down too fast. Dillon was looking at her as if what she had said was the perfect explanation. Maybe it was. She didn't talk to the majority of her friends about her situation and they didn't ask. It was as if the last three years hadn't even happened.

"I thought you said you drew the line at the better-or-worse part?" Callie asked, trying to shake her melancholy.

Dillon laughed. "As a matter of fact, I did. But since all I've learned is your first name, that rule doesn't count."

Callie finally smiled and felt warm inside. She knew nothing about this woman, and she was reacting to her every mood like she was connected to her.

"All right. But tell me when you get bored." Callie expected a flippant remark, and when Dillon didn't say anything she began.

"Three years ago two men broke into my house. My brother Michael was staying with me at the time while his apartment was being fumigated. He heard the commotion and came into my bedroom and saw the men pounding on me." Callie took a sip of her coffee, wondering when the pain of what happened that night would go away. "To make a long story short, Michael beat up the guys, and as a result one of them died. He was convicted of second-degree murder and sentenced to forty years in Lompak prison. The jury obviously didn't care that the men were beating the shit out of me or that one of them was seconds away from raping me. Forty years. They gave my brother forty years for saving my life." Callie felt the weight of her words settle on her shoulders.

"I've been trying to get his conviction appealed but it costs money, a lot of money. So I'm broke, working two jobs to pay the legal fees, and exhausted. My best friend, who begged me to meet her at the Incognito, by the way, stood me up. And to top it all off, I humiliated myself in front of the only woman who's given me more than the time of day in months." Callie stopped and looked upward. She felt as if she had been reading from a long list of woes that hung in midair somewhere above her head, like a black cloud. "That's about it."

Dillon drew on her experience, trying not to display any outward sign of emotion. She hadn't expected Callie to literally dump everything out on the table and was surprised at her own reaction. As Callie had rattled off each of her challenges Dillon's stomach sank, and by the time Callie reached the end, it seemed to have dropped to the floor. *Jesus, what a bunch of shit this lady has on her plate.*

This endless tale of suffering reinforced her gut reaction, telling her to leave this woman and her megaproblems. First of all, she didn't have time for this mess, and secondly, she always bowed out, sometimes not so gracefully, at the first sign of what she termed *issues.* She wasn't interested in someone else's problems. She had enough to deal with at work and didn't want a woman who couldn't keep her own life straightened out. That was why her relationships were sexually fulfilling, yet brief.

She studied Callie across the table. She wasn't at all what Dillon had expected. She held her head high, and for the first time since the I-want-to-fuck-you disaster, Callie was looking directly at her. Her gaze didn't waver. As a matter of fact, a flicker of defiance in her eyes seemed to say, "You asked for it." Dillon guessed Callie's age at forty-two, which made her about eight years older than Dillon. Her face had a few lines—from the stress she was under, no doubt—but bore no other sign of her age.

After a few moments of silence Dillon finally spoke. "I can't believe I'm the only woman who's given you the time of day in months." She echoed Callie's words. "You're beautiful. Men and women would fall all over themselves to get to you."

Callie was shocked at Dillon's response. She had expected her to stumble for an excuse and dash out the door as quickly as possible, but instead she complimented her? Dillon was the most unusual, yet interesting woman she'd met in a long time. She herself was stunning. Her hair was almost jet black with thick waves, one of which kept falling across her forehead. A few streaks of gray were evident, and Callie pegged her in her mid-thirties. Her eyes, which had looked black in the darkness of the bar, were in fact gray and held no sign of pity, only the expectation of a reply.

"No, I'm not." Callie shook her head. "I've got circles under my eyes, lost at least ten pounds, and developed a huge intolerance for practically everything. And somewhere in the past three years I've lost my temper. I've looked everywhere for it, but I have no idea where it is."

Dillon's heart fluttered when a small smile transformed Callie's mouth. She sipped her coffee, giving herself a chance to calm down. "Thanks for the warning, and at the risk of you ripping my head off, I disagree. You're a very beautiful woman. You do look a little tired, but it's"—Dillon glanced at her watch—"eleven thirty on a Friday night. Everyone's tired."

"Then what are you doing here?" Callie asked, almost defensively.

"Chatting with a charming, funny woman."

Callie laughed, involuntarily, it seemed. "Well, I guess if I can't find my temper, it's good that my humor and charm haven't deserted me."

"Would you like to have dinner with me tomorrow night?" Dillon almost glanced around to see who had spoken. She had no idea she was going to say that. It was her turn to feel awkward. Callie searched her eyes as if she were looking for the hidden meaning of life.

"I don't think so."

"Why not?"

"For the reasons I outlined a few minutes ago. I've got too much shit going on in my life, and I'm sure you don't want any part of it."

"I'm not planning to take ownership of your problems or solve them for you. It's just dinner. If I didn't want to see you again, I wouldn't have asked. Believe it or not, I *am* capable of giving a woman the brush-off."

Callie laughed. "Yes, I expect you do have lots of experience in that area." *And other areas as well.*

"I think I've just been complimented."

Dillon frowned, her forehead creasing, and Callie wanted to reach out and smooth the tight lines. "You were—I mean, I did. You're a very attractive woman in a roguish kind of way. I'm sure you could have any woman you choose," she stammered.

"I don't think I'd go that far. You told me no." Dillon looked surprised.

"Ah, but you told me no first." Callie had relaxed and was enjoying their teasing.

"I thought we weren't going to talk about that."

"No, I said that you were not to bring it up. I can," Callie stated, trying to keep her grin from spreading.

"Oh, I get it now. Sometimes I'm a little dense on the nuances of things." They grew quiet for a few minutes before Dillon asked quietly, "Will you reconsider?"

Callie wanted to. It had been eons since she had been out to dinner, and something told her a meal with Dillon wouldn't be at the local Italian restaurant. She wanted to learn more about her. What she did, what she liked, what she thought about world peace—everything and nothing. Callie wanted a normal existence. She missed her life, the one she had before the two men broke into her house and ruined it and that of her brother. It was only one dinner. What harm could it do?

Plenty. It would make her realize just how unhappy she was, that's what it would do. If she let herself experience a sense of normalcy, even for just one evening, she would crave it even more. No, abstinence was the only way she could cope. Maybe after Michael was free she would be able to get on with her life. She shook her head.

"I'm sorry, Dillon. I don't think it's a good idea." She was devoid of emotion.

Chapter Four

I don't care what they want. I own the building. My vote is bigger." Dillon shifted her attention from Greg to the next folder in the stack on her desk. They were reviewing the lease applications for a property she had purchased several years ago and recently remodeled.

"Dillon, Carlson Bakery has been in this location for three generations."

"All the more reason for them to want to stay." Dillon closed the folder that contained the neatly printed application from the family bakery.

"Dillon—" Greg said.

"If they don't want to abide by the signage requirement, the answer is no. I don't care how long they've been there, what they sell, or how many children they're supporting. I don't care. I do care about the property, what it looks like, and my reputation. Other than that I *do not care*," Dillon snapped at Greg.

This wasn't the first meeting where she had flexed her muscle with a tenant. Her properties had a certain look, and she was determined to keep her designs pure.

"What about Dennis Shore?"

"What about him?" Dillon recognized the name of the man from whom she had bought a different piece of property earlier that month.

"He's not happy with the purchase price."

"So what? He signed the papers and cashed my check. If he had a problem with the sale, he shouldn't have signed."

Shore, a gentleman in his late eighties, was the original owner of a house located on a prominent corner downtown. His wife had died suddenly, and the day he put the house up for sale Dillon happened to be driving by on her way to work. She immediately stopped and made him an offer. She had lowballed him just to see his reaction and then forced herself to contain her surprise when he accepted immediately. The price was far less than the property was worth, and she realized that he might not be aware of what he had done, but when the required seven-day cooling-off period had passed, she moved ahead.

"His grandson is making noise."

"Too bad. If he thought ol' Grandpap had diminished capacity, he should have said something in the beginning, not three weeks after the ink has dried." Dillon held up her hand to prevent Greg from speaking. "End of discussion, Greg. What's next?"

Dillon's phone rang and Greg answering it, saying a few words before he handed the receiver to Dillon. "It's Bill Franklin," he said, setting a cup of black coffee on Dillon's desk and dropping back into the chair across from her. "He wants to talk to you specifically to confirm dinner."

Dillon looked up from the single sheet of paper she had been reading all morning. However, she couldn't remember a word she'd seen, which contributed to her short temper. It had been a over week since she and Callie had shared a dance and a cup of coffee. It felt like forever.

Their cup of coffee had turned into three, and they had talked for another hour after Callie turned down her dinner invitation. They walked back to Callie's car in silence, and Dillon had wanted to kiss her good night. Callie must have read her mind because she quickly unlocked the door and got inside.

Dillon had thought of Callie often since watching her pull out of the parking lot. She was disappointed when Callie wouldn't eat with her. Actually, she was more than disappointed. She wanted to spend more time with Callie, but she had never begged a woman to be with her.

Seeing that Greg wasn't about to leave, she punched a button on the phone. "Good morning, Mr. Franklin. It's Dillon Matthews."

"Ms. Matthews, it's good to finally talk with you." Bill Franklin's voice boomed into the office through the speaker phone.

"Yes, it is, and please, call me Dillon."

"And you must call me Bill. All this formality is nothing but a waste of time for a man my age."

"Everything I've read and seen about you, Bill, indicates you're the picture of health." Dillon rolled her eyes at Greg, who was grinning at her.

"My wife is looking forward to Saturday night. She loves playing hostess. She's invited a few other couples, a small dinner-party kind of thing, you know. I hope you don't mind."

Dillon grimaced. She absolutely hated these command performances. She thought she would be with Franklin one-on-one and would seal the deal that evening. She was wrong. "No, not at all. I'm looking forward to it as well." She tossed a paperclip at Greg, who held his hand over his mouth stifling a laugh at her lie.

"Good, good, Phyllis will be so pleased. Your assistant did tell you to bring someone?"

Dillon detected a slight emphasis on the word "someone." "Yes, he did. He said dinner is at seven?" Dillon wanted to divert the topic away from her yet-to-be-decided date.

"Actually dinner is at seven thirty, but everyone will be arriving around seven for drinks. Feel free to come any time." Franklin hesitated and Dillon didn't fill the space. "Um, Dillon, I hate to ask, but Phyllis insisted I find out the name of the person you'll be bringing. Place cards or something like that," he said vaguely.

Dillon felt Greg's eyes on her, probably on full alert for her answer. She hadn't yet determined who she would ask and didn't know why she hadn't called any one of a number of women, so she thought quickly of a response. "Callie." Yes, Callie would be perfect. She was desperate for some attention, and Dillon was confident she could persuade her to go with her. She would be ideal, even though she didn't look a thing like June Cleaver.

"Wonderful." Dillon could almost see the smile in Franklin's voice. "We'll expect to see you and Callie next week, then."

Dillon didn't pay any attention to Bill's sign-off because she was already thinking two steps ahead. "Greg, get me the address of a flower shop in town called Cramer or King or something like that."

"But you always use Royal Florist," he countered, getting up.

"I don't need to order flowers. My date works there."

❖

"Callie, honey, what is wrong with you lately, girl? You can't seem to think straight. No pun intended, hon."

The voice of Callie's boss came from over her right shoulder, and she knew he had caught her daydreaming again. It had been a long week and an even longer weekend, and she had to shake this constant thinking about Dillon. Everywhere she went she looked for dark curly hair. Every time the bell above the door of the flower shop chimed, she glanced up in anticipation of Dillon walking through the door. She fell into bed exhausted and even then couldn't stop seeing the soft gray eyes.

"Sorry, Ross, just a little distracted, that's all." She busied herself with the arrangement she was putting together. It was a simple corsage and she could do it in her sleep. But between her jobs and traveling three hours each way every week to see Michael, sleep wasn't high on her list of priorities.

"What's up, Callie? I know you're worried about Michael, but he's a smart guy. He knows what he has to do to be safe in there. He'll be okay. You need to take care of yourself for a change."

Callie carefully set a rose on the counter and hugged Ross. "I know, I know," she said, sighing. "I'm trying. I did go out last weekend." She didn't tell him that it was only to meet Audrey, and other than talking to Dillon she had had a terrible time. She didn't want Ross to know that Dillon had sidetracked her attention. More than once she had kicked herself for turning down Dillon's dinner invitation, but she knew it was the right thing to do. She couldn't handle getting involved with someone right now.

"Do tell," Ross demanded excitedly.

"It was no big deal. I went to the Incognito, had a few beers, danced a little, and went home. Alone," she added at Ross's expectant look.

"That's it?"

"That's about it." Callie knew Ross wanted her to have met someone and been swept off her feet. He was an old queen and wanted everyone to be as happy as he and John were.

"Callie, honey, when was the last time you got laid?"

She couldn't help but laugh. Ross was one of those people who thought sex was the cure for anything from depression to sore feet, and everything in between.

"You probably know that better than I, Ross."

"Hmm, I think it was sometime in 2006—the spring, I think."

Callie loved Ross's sense of humor, and she could always count on him to chase away the blues. She was still laughing when the front door opened.

She glanced up and her laugh stuck in her throat. Dillon stood on the threshold staring right at her with an expression she remembered from the dance floor. Actually, she remembered it every night when she closed her eyes. She grabbed the counter for support as Dillon moved closer.

"Hi," Callie said tentatively.

"Hi." Dillon found her voice from somewhere. The other night, Callie hadn't laughed like she had when Dillon entered the flower shop. The sound was full and deep and tickled the inside of her stomach. She pushed it aside, intent on her plan. "I hope you don't mind that I stopped by," she asked, glancing around the shop.

The man standing next to Callie nudged her. "No, no, it's fine," she stammered. "How did you find me?"

"Google," she replied. She looked back and forth from the obviously gay man to Callie. "Will you be taking a break soon? I'd like to talk to you. I can wait in the car until—"

The man, who Dillon assumed was the owner, interrupted her.

"She was about to when you walked in. Callie, go ahead. I'll hold down the fort." He gently pushed Callie in Dillon's direction.

Dillon stepped aside and held the door as they walked out. "Would you like to get something to drink?" She gestured to the snack shop two doors down.

The flower shop was located in a strip mall surrounded by an Italian deli on the left and an insurance office on the right. Earlier, when Greg gave her the shop's address, she recognized it as one of her properties. Several years before now, the strip mall had been dilapidated, and after buying out the leases of the current occupants, she had extensively remodeled it inside and out. Some of the original occupants wanted to return but Dillon declined, desiring a more elite clientele in the property.

"Sure."

They settled in two chairs on the snack shop's patio, each sipping a cold drink.

When Dillon had walked into the shop, at first Callie thought she was dreaming. But she was recovering now, and her mind was beginning to function.

"It's good to see you again." She wasn't sure why Dillon was here.

After a pause, Dillon said, "You too. I've been thinking about you. I know you told me you didn't want to go out to dinner with me, but I'd like to ask a favor instead."

"A favor?" What on earth kind of favor could she do for a woman she barely knew?

"I need a date," Dillon said.

"*You* need a date? Come on, Dillon, you can get a date anywhere." Her heart was still pounding at the thought that Dillon had come to her. Dillon lifted the cup to her lips, and Callie watched every inch of the movement. She had sensed that Dillon wanted to kiss her the other night, and she had wanted to be kissed. So why did she dive into her car like a teenager?

"Yeah, well, let me start over. I've been invited to a dinner party this weekend, and I'd like for you to accompany me."

Dillon tried not to peek at her watch. She had dozens of things to do today, and she hoped trying to convince Callie, when any of a dozen other women would say yes, wasn't a waste of time.

"A dinner party?"

"Yes. The hosts are Bill Franklin and his wife. I'm trying to buy some property from him and he suggested we meet in a more social atmosphere. It's Saturday. Are you free?" Dillon vaguely remembered Callie mentioning something about a second job, but she couldn't recall exactly what.

Callie quickly ran through the calendar in her brain. She was scheduled to work the day shift on her second job and would be off by five o'clock. Most weekends the only things she had going were laundry and visiting Michael. However, she wanted to keep an escape route if something happened that might sway her one way or the other.

"I think I'm available. I'll have to check, though. Why did you ask? I told you it wouldn't be a good idea for us to go out."

"You did, but we're not going out. We're going to a party."

"What's the difference?" Callie hadn't seen this invitation coming. She thought Dillon would invite her to something a little more intimate, not something involving a group of people.

"Well, one concerns just you and me, and the other entails a room full of people."

Dillon's dimples deepened, and Callie was drawn into them just as she was the first time she saw them. "I know the difference between two people having dinner and a party."

"I thought maybe you just didn't want to be alone with me, so this way you have the safety of numbers." Dillon looked at her empty glass and signaled the waiter for a refill.

"Should I be afraid to be alone with you?" Callie didn't think so, and she was generally a good judge of character.

The waiter refilled their glasses with tea, and Dillon tore open two sweetener packets. "No, not at all. I just thought you might be more comfortable with other people around."

The clinking of the teaspoon in Dillon's glass was almost hypnotic. "I'm not afraid to be alone with you. I said I didn't think it was a good idea that we went out."

Dillon fought down her irritation. This wasn't going as she had planned. "Look, Callie, we all have some sort of baggage. For some of us it's Gucci and for others it's Samsonite. Either way, it doesn't matter. We all have some. I will admit that yours is a bit more interesting than most, but that doesn't make me not want to have dinner with you."

Dillon wasn't getting any traction, so she changed her approach. "Callie, it's just dinner. I won't know anyone there other than you. We can form a united front. Make people think we've known each other for years. Heck, maybe even pretend we're madly in love." Callie's head popped up at her last statement. "Come on, let's have some fun."

"All right, I'll go."

"Great. Franklin lives in Westwood Estates, so I'm sure it's a dressy kind of thing." She pulled out a pen and passed it and a napkin to Callie. "Write down your address and I'll pick you up around six thirty. Drinks at seven, dinner at seven thirty."

Dillon contained her sigh of relief as Callie wrote her address on the napkin. Part one of her plan was complete. Well, it was at least penciled in. Something could happen between now and Saturday night, and if it did she would fall back on plan B. However, she was confident she wouldn't need a plan B.

Callie was still smiling when Dillon left her at the door of the shop. Ross was waiting for her inside and she knew he would grill her. She wasn't up to twenty questions so she preempted them.

"Her name is…" She hesitated as she looked at the name embossed in gold on the business card Dillon had given her, with her cell phone number jotted down on the back in case Callie needed to contact her. "Dillon Matthews, and I met her the other night. We danced a few songs, had a cup of coffee, chatted for a while, and I never expected to see her again. She asked me to go to a dinner party with her, I agreed, and there's nothing more to say."

"Dillon Matthews?" Ross asked.

"Yes." Callie answered hesitantly. Ross had that look in his eyes he got when he was on to something. She handed him the business card.

"Dillon Matthews owns this building. Shit, she owns the entire block."

Ross took the card from Callie and turned it over in his pudgy fingers. He whistled. "Very nice, classy."

Callie's stomach lurched. "What? Christ, I had no idea who she was. She said she planned to buy some property from the man who's having the dinner party, but it was more a social occasion than anything else."

Ross handed the card back to her. "I hope you have something very nice to wear, because I don't think it will be your everyday affair." He moved behind the counter again and began to tie a red ribbon around the neck of a vase.

Callie groaned. Her wardrobe consisted primarily of jeans, Dockers, and two pairs of dress slacks, none of which was appropriate for what she imagined the evening would require. Her Visa card was almost maxed out, but maybe, just maybe she could squeeze out another couple of hundred for the black dress she saw on sale a few days ago at Saks.

"What's a woman like Dillon Matthews doing in a bar like the Incog?"

The shortened version of the name of the bar where she met Dillon pulled Callie back from the inside of her closet. "What did you say?"

"I said that Dillon could have her pick of women. She's rich and a knockout. If I were a lesbian, I'd be after her. Why is she going to the Incog to get a date?"

"Ross," Callie said. "Jeez, it sounds like you think every woman that goes there is desperate and can't get a date anywhere else. What does that say about me? I was there."

Like all bars, the Incognito had its share of women who drank too much and were looking for love in all the wrong places, but she had often seen couples who simply wanted to get out for a night with their friends and go dancing. Callie knew it wasn't the best place to find someone, but she had met her share of losers in the grocery store as well.

"Oh, no, sweetie." Ross began to recover from his snafu.

"That's not what I meant at all. Perfectly good people go to bars, but you have to admit they're few and far between. I was just wondering what she was doing there." The phone rang and his attention was immediately diverted.

Callie had to admit she had wondered the same thing. Why was Dillon there? Callie had assumed she was looking for some casual sex, but when Callie offered, she declined. Dillon obviously found her attractive, and even though Callie might not have wanted to have sex with her, Dillon obviously didn't think she was a beast. She had invited her to dinner and tracked her down to ask her to a party. A social gathering where everyone would know she was Dillon's date. Dillon was intriguing, and for the first time in a long while, Callie had something to look forward to.

But she was wary, also. She returned to the corsage she had abandoned. Why would someone like Dillon pursue her? Her resolve had faded far too easily under Dillon's charm when she invited her to the dinner party. The rose Callie had been about to use in the corsage had wilted, so she chose another one. If Dillon was always this persuasive, Callie would have to be careful because she could very easily fall for her. In fact, she felt as if she had just stepped off a cliff into a deep ravine with no bottom in sight.

CHAPTER FIVE

The road to Lompak symbolized the isolation of the prison itself. Callie could see for miles in every direction, but the only way to get anywhere was to stay on the long, straight highway that never seemed to end. The drive there usually took three hours, and she had made this trip so many times she had memorized practically every road sign.

She dreaded these visits with her brother. Her heart ached when she saw him wasting away in such a cold, hard place, where hatred grew daily. He was clearly trying to hide the details of his existence in close proximity with eight thousand men with nothing but time, and occasionally each other, to kill, but she had to do something. Michael was her brother. He had saved her from a vicious attack, possibly worse. She always left feeling sad and angry. She stayed depressed for two or three days afterward, and just when she began to feel better she got back on the road to Lompak. In some ways she was as trapped as Michael, but there was absolutely no comparison.

Callie pulled into the large parking lot and into a spot in the first row. The lot was usually full when she arrived, but today was Friday, obviously not a high-volume visiting day. She signed her name three times, showed her identification four times, had her purse searched twice, and was finally seated on a hard round stool bolted to the floor. The thick glass that separated her from her brother was scratched, and several people had carved their initials into the counter near where her hands now rested.

The seat to her left was empty, but a woman with an ass too large for the stool sat to her right. Even though she was practically shouting into the phone she held in her chubby hand, Callie could barely understand what she was saying. Something about his "sorry ass" and her having to get a job while he sat on his butt all day playing cards and talking smack. Callie wondered why the man on the other side of the glass even agreed to see her if all she did was give him shit. She suspected if he refused he would be in even deeper shit when he got out.

Michael came in, an expectant look on his face, and sat gingerly on the stool across from her. His black hair had been cut short and his complexion was paler than a week ago. She reached for the phone that hung limply on the thick partition and gave a mocking illusion of privacy. The handset was sticky, and she tried not to think out what germ or bodily fluid she was touching.

On her first visit she pulled a travel-size bottle of hand sanitizer from her purse and wiped down the phone that was in a similarly disgusting condition. Michael immediately told her never to do it again, as it would cause him problems. The other inmates would think she considered herself better than everyone else, simply because of her hygienic actions, and because she was his sister, he would get the reputation as well. She gritted her teeth, thinking about the large bottle of disinfectant waiting for her in the car.

"Hey, buddy." She greeted Michael with her favorite nickname for him.

"Hi, Callie. What are you doing here today?" She typically visited him on Saturday, unless she had some news regarding his appeal.

"Can't I come visit my brother when I want to?"

Michael's voice softened a little and he dropped his sad brown eyes. "You know I don't want you to see me like this."

He had been trying to convince her to stop visiting him. She always ignored him and prayed he wouldn't make her promise not to come again or, worse yet, refuse to enter the visitation room when she did make the trip.

"Michael, I love you. You're my brother, and you're here because of me." This was her sentence too.

"For God's sake, Callie. When are you going to get over this? It's not your fault those two creeps broke into your house, or that they broke your nose and hit you so hard your eardrum burst, or that Miller smacked his head on the edge of the nightstand and died. You aren't to blame for anything, and you certainly aren't responsible for my actions. How many times do we have to have this argument?" His voice grew louder as he spoke.

Callie knew Michael was right, but more than reinforced glass separated them now. He had enough crap to deal with. He didn't need her guilt as well. She reached down and turned up her positive-attitude meter.

"I have a date tomorrow night."

His eyes slowly lit up. He had been badgering her to get on with her life, and his reaction clearly showed his joy that she had done just that. On previous visits she had thought about lying to him, but she respected him enough not to.

"Well, it's about time. Tell me about her."

Callie smiled as she thought of Dillon. "She's funny, smart, and confident without being arrogant, and very polite."

"And?" her brother prompted.

"She's hot. I mean really hot. Her body looks like it was sculpted from marble with all the right muscles and curves in all the right places. She's got dimples when she smiles and the grayest eyes I've ever seen." Callie felt herself blush.

"Now, that's what I wanted to know." For the first time in months, Michael laughed.

Callie spent the next twenty minutes sharing her life with him. They talked about the flower shop, her boss, and Dillon. The one thing they didn't talk about was his case. Michael had told Callie that if she didn't have any good news about his appeal, he didn't want to hear anything at all.

He was the first person she told when she realized she was a lesbian, and he had been her biggest supporter ever since. They would go out together and cruise girls, teasing each other about not having to compete for the same girl. Michael preferred blondes with a few extra pounds on them, and Callie was attracted to dark-haired, strong women.

The buzzer rang in her ear, signaling she had only five minutes before their time was up. The prison policy allowed no more than thirty minutes per visitation. After that, the line went dead whether they had finished their conversation or not.

At the one-minute mark the buzzer rang again, and she told Michael how much she loved him and thought about him every day. She promised to describe her date in detail and begged him to be careful. She had just finished when she heard the familiar dead silence on the line. They sat there for a minute before the guard tapped Michael on the shoulder, indicating it was time for him to leave. Again by mutual agreement, Callie left the room first.

She managed to keep her tears in check through the exit processing, and only when she was in the safety of her locked car did she let them spill onto her cheeks. She could hardly bear the pain of seeing Michael in such a horrendous situation. Her father had left when Michael was a child, and her mother had her own demons to bear. At times like this she felt as if it were her and Michael against the world.

Callie often wished she had settled down earlier and had someone in her life to help. She had a lot of good friends who were her support system, but they weren't the same as a partner. A woman who loved her, who would be there for her no matter what she needed. The weight of what she was up against constantly wore on her, but Michael depended on her and she wouldn't let him down.

CHAPTER SIX

The house Dillon was looking for was the next one on the left, and she turned on her blinker and pulled into the wide drive. Callie's neighborhood was a little run-down, but the yards were neat and free of clutter. The residents obviously had pride in their homes, if not a lot of money. The recently cut grass in Callie's yard was trimmed to razor-sharp edges. The flower bed running parallel to the driveway was lush, and the smell of fresh gardening mulch filled Dillon's nostrils when she stepped out of the car. The click, click of the cooling engine mimicked the sound of her heels tapping on the sidewalk as she approached the front door. She pushed the doorbell, suddenly nervous.

She had been so busy at work that she hardly had a chance to think about this evening with Callie. She had to make a last-minute trip to San Francisco and would have been late tonight if her flight had been delayed any longer. Dillon hated flying commercial, preferring to charter whenever possible. The time it saved her from waiting in security lines and sitting in airports or on the tarmac was "priceless," as the Visa card commercial said.

The front door opened and for a moment Dillon wasn't sure the woman standing in front of her was the same one she'd asked out. June Cleaver she was not. Callie was absolutely dazzling. Her hair was up and away from her face, revealing high cheekbones lightly brushed with makeup. Her blue eyes were bright, clear, and so refreshing Dillon wanted to drown in them. She was wearing a plain black dress held up by straps no thicker than a piano wire. Her shoulders were tan and begged to be caressed. The dress accentuated the curves and planes of her body as if it were made specifically for her. By the time Dillon's gaze traveled up Callie's body she was met with a look that was part relief that Dillon liked what she saw and annoyance that she had looked at her like that at all.

"I'm sorry for staring. But you are absolutely gorgeous."

"Thank you. Please come in. I have to grab one more thing and then I'll be ready." Callie caught a hint of Dillon's cologne and recognized it as the one her brother used to wear. She liked it on him and really liked it on her. "Do you want something to drink?" When Dillon shook her head she said, "Please make yourself at home. I'll just be a minute."

She left Dillon in the living room and walked down the hall toward the bedroom. Once inside her knees almost gave out and she practically fell on the bed. She really didn't need anything other than a minute to pull herself back together. Dillon was the most attractive woman she had ever seen. The clothes she had on at the bar did nothing for her compared to the tan trousers, pale blue shirt, and navy jacket she now wore, all of which Callie suspected were made of raw silk. Tall and elegant and decidedly butch, she was androgynous yet feminine enough to pull off either look with ease. Audrey would say that she was absolutely yummy. Callie had another word for it. Stunning.

It had been almost three years since she had even looked at a woman, and longer than that since she had felt a woman's touch. Her senses awakened in an explosion that surprised her. She took a few deep breaths to calm her racing heart and grabbed her red shawl for both warmth and a splash of color.

Meanwhile, Dillon gravitated toward the paintings mounted on the wall on either side of the fireplace. They were bright and vibrant, filled with color and light. She preferred impressionist art such as this because she could see something entirely new each time she looked at it. These were good, very good. She leaned closer to see the artist's name and shot her eyebrows up.

"I'm ready."

"Is this you?" Dillon pointed at the signature on the painting.

"Yes. I dabble a little here and there, though I haven't touched a paintbrush recently."

"I'd say this is more than just dabbling. This is good. Really good." Dillon wasn't a connoisseur of art but she knew what she liked, and she liked this. She wondered if Callie had any more.

"Thanks," Callie replied, and hung her head, as if she was embarrassed.

"No, I mean it. Do you have any on display? Do you sell?" Dillon was uncharacteristically rambling.

"I've given a few to my friends, but it's just a hobby. Another outlet for my creative juices." She was starting to look uncomfortable with the way Dillon was admiring her work. "I'm ready."

If Callie weren't so beautiful, Dillon could look at these paintings for hours. They created a sense of peacefulness she hadn't felt in some time. When she was a child her mother took her to the art museum twice a week for their summer program, and Dillon begged her to let her go every day. Her father thought the lessons were a waste of time and money, and said as much on more than one occasion, calling painting frivolous and not a respectable profession, but her mother took her anyway. At one time she wanted to go to art school but knew she would never be able to afford to live if she did. She had no desire to be a starving artist. Architecture was a close second.

The drive to Westwood Estates took twenty minutes and Dillon's car was more than comfortable. Callie had never been in a BMW, let alone a 750 series, and she added this car to the list of what she would buy if and when she won the lottery.

"You didn't tell me you were *the* Dillon Matthews."

"It doesn't sound like you're impressed."

"Are you trying to impress me?"

"If I were trying to, I would have told you who I was the first time we met. I would have taken you to the Cedars for coffee and picked you up tonight in my Hummer."

"You have a Hummer?" Callie was more interested in the gas-guzzling vehicle than the most expensive restaurant in the city.

"Of course I do. I'm a lesbian and I'm rich. What else would I have?"

"A Jaguar," Callie threw out jokingly. She was surprised at the expression on Dillon's face. "You have a Hummer and a Jaguar?" Callie wondered again just how and why she was sitting next to a woman who spent more money on one car than Callie made in a year, maybe two.

"If I say yes, will you count it against me?"

"What color is it?" Callie asked mischievously.

"Emerald fire," Dillon answered without hesitation.

"Emerald fire?" Callie laughed. "So what color is it really?"

"Green."

Callie nodded. "Good Lord. Why is it that the more expensive the car, the more ridiculous the names of the color? I mean, how many shades of green are there?"

She stopped, suddenly aware that what she said might offend Dillon. She tried to think of something to smooth over her critical comment but came up empty.

Dillon felt the tension in the air as the car turned into the drive of the luxury community. Normally she would have snapped back a retort that would have put anyone who dared talk to her like that in their place. But as the guard stepped out of the large building that separated the residents of Westwood Estates from the commoners, Dillon calmed down. She needed Callie tonight, and it would not be in her best interest if they arrived on the Franklins' doorstep arguing.

"Emerald fire does sound a bit pompous, doesn't it?" The tension left the car as Dillon rolled down her window and gave the guard her name. As he checked his clipboard and retreated inside the building, Dillon thought of the care she'd taken not to try to impress Callie when they first met. Too many people sucked up to her when they found out who she was, and Dillon wanted things to be different with Callie. *Well, I certainly got my wish.* Within seconds, the gate opened and Dillon roused from her reverie and drove through.

Callie had never seen houses as large as the ones they passed on the tree-lined streets. Each one sat back from the street far enough for the occupants not to hear any noise from traffic but not too far to be hidden from view. The soft voice of the navigation system directed them around the next corner and told them the address they were looking for was one hundred feet ahead on their right. Dillon turned into a wide driveway, the BMW's suspension absorbing the shock of the brick-laid surface. She pulled to a stop near the front door and turned off the engine. Leaning forward, she tilted her head and looked at the mansion through the windshield.

"Nice digs."

"I'll say."

Callie was shocked at the size of the house and nervous that she was going to a party inside it. What did she have in common with these people? Nothing, other than the fact that she might have designed a floral arrangement that had been delivered here. But this was not the clientele that Crane Florist typically serviced.

Dillon must have sensed her apprehension because her hand was suddenly covered by a large warm one. "You'll be fine. You look great. One glance and everyone will be gaga over you. If you run out of things to say, give me the high sign and I'll come rescue you. Better yet, stay beside me. That way you won't have to worry, and I'll have the prettiest woman in the room on my arm."

Callie froze. "Dillon, do these people know you're a lesbian?"

Dillon squeezed her hand reassuringly. "Yes, they do. Bill Franklin specifically asked me to bring a date. As a matter of fact, he almost insisted on it. Don't worry. He wants this deal as much as I do. He won't do anything to jeopardize it." Dillon let go of her hand, and Callie faintly noticed how cold and empty it felt.

"Come on. Let's go inside." Dillon reached for the door knocker.

❖

Dillon was used to houses as elegant as Bill Franklin's and recognized the work of a few familiar artists hanging on the walls surrounding them. A man clad in a tuxedo had answered the door and promptly welcomed them inside, and their footsteps echoed in the large foyer.

She hesitated in the doorway to the gigantic living room, preferring to get the lay of the land, so to speak, before venturing any farther. Naturally guarded, Dillon used the opportunity to put names to faces she recognized. She knew a few of them, but most she did not. She reviewed a mental checklist of what she needed to accomplish tonight. Her top priority was to get Bill Franklin to sign over his property to her. Simple. Piece of cake. She would have him in her back pocket before the night was half over. She grasped Callie's hand and stepped forward, then stopped abruptly.

"Dillon, I'm Bill Franklin. It's a pleasure to meet you."

"Mr. Frank…" Dillon stopped and corrected herself as she accepted the hand offered to her. "Bill, yes, it is a pleasure."

"This is my wife, Phyllis."

Dillon dropped his hand and extended hers to the woman who was at least five inches taller than her husband. "Phyllis, you have a lovely home."

"Thank you, Dillon. It's a bit much for me, but I'll pass your compliment on to my decorator."

Dillon detected a sadness in Phyllis Franklin's eyes that for some reason troubled her. She couldn't pinpoint exactly what might have caused it, but of course she had just met the woman. Brushing it off, she turned to bring Callie closer to her side. "May I introduce Callie Sheffield."

Callie was grateful for Dillon's lead. The opulence in the room overwhelmed her so completely she had been unsure if she could put one foot in front of the other on her own. Everywhere she looked, the furnishings screamed money. Her shoes sank in carpet so thick she was tempted to remove them and confirm she was indeed standing on clouds.

Bill greeted her first. "Callie, I'm glad you could join us. My wife and I have been looking forward to this evening all week."

His hand was warm and strong, and Callie felt immediately at home. "Thank you for inviting me, Mr. Franklin." She was cut off by their host insisting she call him Bill. "And Phyllis, thank you for having me as well."

"It's my pleasure, dear. We see the same old people party after party. Bill so seldom invites anyone of interest. It's good to see new faces in the house."

"Come in, ladies. What can I get you to drink?" Bill asked.

They placed their drink order and Phyllis immediately began to introduce them to the rest of the guests. By the time dinner was served, Dillon had met two investment bankers, an attorney, two bored wives, and one half-drunk husband who couldn't keep his eyes off Callie.

Callie had kept up her share of the conversation and Dillon was impressed with how easily she talked with people. Even though Callie stayed near her, it appeared to Dillon that her nervousness had disappeared and she was enjoying herself.

At the table, Callie sat on Dillon's left with Phyllis on her right. The leering husband was directly across from Callie and his eyes were permanently affixed to her chest. Callie didn't indicate she was aware of the attention. In fact, she tried to engage the man in conversation but stopped when it was apparent he had nothing to say. Phyllis dominated most of the conversation and at one point asked, "So, Callie, how long have you and Dillon been seeing each other?"

Callie almost dropped her fork, and Dillon tensed and waited anxiously for Callie's response. Even though this was technically their first date, she didn't want to share that piece of information with anyone.

"For a while now," Callie answered vaguely.

Dillon had nearly choked on the bite of broccoli she was chewing but, somewhat relieved, she resumed eating. She hadn't considered that the conversation might go down this path. She had been to so many of these business dinners masked as social events that she hadn't even assumed this one was anything different. She hadn't told Callie much about the situation, and it would have been embarrassing if the Franklins discovered they were practically strangers. She searched Callie's face for some sign of what she was up to, and when she found nothing she frowned. Why was she making her look good?

"Come on, you two, don't be shy. After all these years I remember the first time I saw Bill like it was yesterday. Where did you meet?" Phyllis directed her question again to Callie.

"At a dance," Callie replied smoothly. "I was waiting for a friend and Dillon asked me to dance."

"And what did you think when she asked?" Phyllis inquired.

Callie hesitated. "Well, actually," Callie cast a knowing glance at Dillon, "I thought she was hitting on me."

"I was not," Dillon interjected in her defense, even though that was exactly her intention.

"You were too," Callie replied, as if she could read Dillon's mind.

"I can understand that, Dillon," Phyllis said. "Callie is a beautiful woman."

Dillon wasn't sure where this conversation was going so she remained cautious. This was unlike any other table talk she'd experienced. "Yes, Phyllis, I couldn't agree with you more. But I wasn't hitting on her."

"Uh-huh," Phyllis added. "You're a scoundrel, Dillon Matthews. I read the papers."

Dillon couldn't help but laugh at the characterization. "A scoundrel?"

Phyllis sipped her coffee. "Yes. A scoundrel, a rogue, you know. My Bill was exactly like you forty years ago. You even have the look, with those dark eyes and brooding expression. You probably have the girls eating out of your hand." Phyllis chuckled.

Callie chimed in. "Not anymore. She's the perfect lady. Never even looks at another woman when we're together." She shifted slightly in her chair, pressing her leg against Dillon's. The contact was meant to signal to Dillon she was teasing, but at the first touch, a wash of heat shot through Callie. This time she did drop her fork.

As she watched Dillon out of the corner of her eye, the wash of heat became a wave.

"Very admirable, Dillon. I guess you're not that bad after all. Bill stopped his shenanigans after he met me too."

Callie was caught up in the light teasing and couldn't help but say, "Obviously, Phyllis, we know what it takes to keep our men and women happy."

Phyllis was clearly hip to the fact that she and Dillon were lesbians and was asking leading questions, so Callie relaxed. But when she considered what she had just said, her mouth suddenly became dry at the thought of keeping Dillon happy. The sex would be intense and powerful. She wanted to know just how intense.

"Amen to that, sister."

Dillon sat in stunned silence. How had the conversation gotten this personal so fast? The way Callie and Phyllis were talking like sorority sisters and glancing at each other like they shared a secret was making her nervous. It was as if they had been having dinner with Phyllis for years, not an hour. Phyllis had a way of making people feel comfortable, as if they were talking to their grandmother or great-aunt. They had known each other for only a few hours, but Dillon felt as if she could tell this woman anything, totally unlike her relationship with her own mother.

"You're awfully quiet, Dillon," Phyllis commented, then added, "It appears as though your woman here has you right where you want to be."

Finally able to say something, Dillon wasn't sure what it should be. If she refuted what Callie had said, then she might damage her chance to close the deal tonight. Shrugging, she replied, "What can I say, Phyllis? You've got me pegged. But please don't tell anyone. I have a reputation to uphold, you know. You said it yourself, you read the papers. Others do as well. A girl can't be too careful." Dillon winked at her as if it were their turn to share a secret.

"Yes, I do. We women keep a few secrets hidden under our skirts."

Dillon choked on her wine and grabbed her napkin before the

red liquid could spill out onto the tablecloth and, most likely, all over her as well. "Very well put, Phyllis. I happen to like what some women hide under their skirts," she murmured under her breath.

Dinner over, they adjourned to the den for dessert and coffee. Phyllis mingled with her other guests but spent most of the evening talking with Callie. Dillon tried on several occasions to pin Bill down, but he kept sidestepping her attempts to talk business.

"Dillon, Callie is absolutely charming."

Dillon sipped her brandy as she and Bill walked through the French door onto the patio. "Thank you. She and Phyllis seem to be hitting it off rather well. They've been inseparable ever since we got here."

"That's what scares me. God knows what we're up against when two women get together."

Bill was talking to her as if they were two men discussing their wives. Well, weren't they? Other than the fact that she barely knew Callie's last name, wasn't that what this was all about?

"I hope my wife's forwardness didn't upset you or Callie. She has yet to master the art of subtle small talk." Bill looked at Dillon as if to say, "You know what I mean."

"I prefer the direct approach. Fortunately, it has served me well in business. Why beat around the bush and waste everybody's time? Why not just come out and say exactly what you want?" This was the perfect opening for her to again approach their business deal. "Bill," she said.

Something in her tone must have indicated business because he immediately deflected her. "I couldn't agree more, Dillon. I like you, and Phyllis is definitely smitten by Callie. We're going to our house on Paradise Island next weekend. I know Phyllis would love it if you two would join us. And if I know my wife, she's probably already asked Callie."

Dillon kept her irritation at the old man to herself. What would it take to get him to discuss her offer, let alone sign the papers? He was a much more formidable businessman than she had been led to believe. She made a mental note to discuss her realization with Greg and the rest of her staff. This would not happen again.

"That sounds wonderful, Bill, but I'll have to talk to Callie. I'm not sure what her plans are." Dillon looked through the doorway and saw Callie and Phyllis laughing. Warmth infused her at the thought of spending more time with Callie, but was almost cooled by her impatience to get her project going. She was losing money every day the equipment to start phase one of Gateway sat idle in a rented lot on the other side of town.

"Excellent," Bill said enthusiastically. "I'll have my assistant call yours and they can work out the details. You've never seen anything as beautiful as you will next week."

Dillon was gazing at Callie, and an image of her lying half naked on the beach filled her brain. Her stomach jumped a little and she had to swallow a lump in her throat that came out of nowhere. "You're probably right."

CHAPTER SEVEN

Despite being nervous, Callie had enjoyed herself this evening, and she had enjoyed watching Dillon even more. Several times throughout the evening she had covertly studied her. Dillon wasn't overly tall, but she carried herself with a sense of authority that came with self-made success. Her body language was the same whether she was talking to a group of men or women. She seemed to respect the opinions of each group and didn't shy away from one or the other. Callie had known a few lesbians who were either intimidated by straight women or wanted to dominate them. Dillon was definitely not one of them, Callie thought as she buckled her seat belt.

Dillon started the car and pulled out of the drive. "I hope you had a good time. Phyllis hardly let you out of her sight."

Callie chuckled. "She said I reminded her of her granddaughter. I did have a good time. I'll admit I was a bit intimidated at first, but the Franklins are wonderful hosts and their friends were nice and warm too."

"I'm glad you feel that way, because Bill invited us to their house in the Bahamas next weekend." Dillon wasn't sure how Callie would react, and she wasn't even sure what she was thinking.

Callie laughed. "They certainly are a tag team. Phyllis invited us as well. She said they have a house on a private beach with sand as white as snow. If their house here is any indication, I'm sure it's magnificent."

Dillon accelerated past a bus in the right lane with an advertisement for the six o'clock news splayed on the side. Should she ask Callie if she wanted to go or just make up an excuse that would let all of them off the hook? "Yeah, they are quite the pair, aren't they? He adores her, that's for sure, and I know who wears the pants in that family."

"As it should be."

Dillon's smile deepened and she faced Callie for a moment before returning her attention to the road. Callie was once again drawn to Dillon's deep dimples. Her stomach twitched and she had to remind herself to be careful of Dillon's charm.

"How does that work between two women?" Callie asked. "I read somewhere that the one who cares the least in a relationship holds all the power." It had taken her a few minutes to grasp that concept when she first heard it, but Dillon seemed to immediately understand.

"That makes sense. The person who has the most to lose will do just about anything not to, whatever it is. It's the same in business. If you want something that someone else has, it's their hoops you'll jump through to get it. Therefore you are definitely not the one in control."

Dillon's insight interested Callie. "Do you think someone always has to be?"

"Don't you? Someone has to be in charge or you just flounder. If you're going out to dinner, one of you needs to make the first recommendation or you'd starve."

"But what about in a relationship?"

"I don't see it as any different," Dillon said matter-of-factly.

"But it's supposed to be give and take, equal." At least that was Callie's idea of how things should be. She wondered if Dillon had been seriously involved with many women and, if so, if she had always been in charge.

"Of course it is, at least in theory. But in every relationship, whether in business or pleasure, someone leads all the time. That leader may change depending on the situation, but someone is always out in front."

"You're used to being the one in command, aren't you?" Callie asked, hoping she didn't sound accusatory by using such a strong word.

"I run a multimillion-dollar business. I'm responsible for hundreds of people and dozens of properties. My name is on the letterhead."

How would Dillon react if she were forced to give up control in her life? For the past three years Callie had absolutely none over hers. She divided her life into before and after the attack. Before, she had plans and was slowly but steadily achieving them. She knew where she wanted to be in five, then ten years. She had friends, a steady girlfriend now and then, and was happy. But now she felt as if she had absolutely no say in anything. She worked because she had to, visited Michael because she had to, spearheaded his defense because she had to. She couldn't remember the last time she did anything just for Callie.

They sat in silence for the remainder of the drive to Callie's house. Dillon was preoccupied with Bill's invitation. If it was important enough to make him decide to finalize this deal, she would accept. She hadn't had a vacation in as long as she could remember, and a few days in the sun sounded wonderful. Why not mix business with pleasure?

"So about their invitation," Dillon said, "I realize we barely know each other, but would you like to go? I can clear my schedule for a few days. I mean, if you don't have to work or anything." To her ears she was rambling and sounded like a schoolgirl. She really wanted Callie to say yes.

However much Callie wanted Dillon to ask her to go, she was surprised at her reaction when she actually did. Her stomach jumped into her throat and her nerves were suddenly alive. "I suppose I could get off. Ross is usually good about that sort of stuff. That, and the fact that since you came to the shop he's dying of curiosity about you. I can withhold information until he says yes." Callie smiled in anticipation of her discussion with Ross on Monday.

She hadn't been anywhere in years except back and forth to Lompak. The name of the prison where her brother was incarcerated brought with it an overwhelming sense of guilt. Why should she have the opportunity to enjoy herself when all he saw of the sun and the sky was within the fifteen-foot walls of his home for the next thirty years? She tried to ignore the question.

Dillon hadn't experienced the sensation of butterflies frolicking around in her stomach in years, and she attributed it to the excitement of getting near the close of this deal. "Okay, I'll have my assistant Greg call Bill on Monday. He said something about Friday to Monday. Have you ever been to the Bahamas?"

"No, have you?"

"Two or three times. All you need to know is that it's warm and sunny. No need for a big wardrobe, but you will need lots of sunscreen." Dillon was already reviewing her schedule for the next week to see what she could possibly move where. Her days typically contained one meeting after another and usually didn't end until long after nine p.m. It would be a bitch to get ready to go and a bigger bitch to catch up once she got back.

Callie was grateful for Dillon's comment about clothes, if nothing else. Her wardrobe was adequate for a few days on the beach, though not much more, and thankfully her swimsuit was in good condition. She had lost weight since she wore it last, but was sure it would still fit. She had a pair of sandals, and a few sundresses for the evenings. As long as they didn't go anywhere fancy, she'd be okay.

She wouldn't have a problem getting the time off from Ross, and it would be her long weekend free from her part-time job. She would have to put in extra hours at the shop to ensure she received a full paycheck, and she had no clue how she would manage that and still make her weekly trip to see Michael. Something would have to give this week, and it would most likely be sleep.

Callie was so engrossed in her thoughts she wasn't aware that Dillon's car was in her driveway with the engine off. A flush of embarrassment heated her face, and she was grateful for the darkness around them. "Sorry, caught me daydreaming."

"Hopefully something good," Dillon said.

"Just making a to-do list for the week, to be ready." Callie tried to make her response light and not signal the intensity of the conflict brewing inside her.

"I know what you mean. I've got a full day of meetings on both Friday and Monday. Greg's going to shoot me when I tell him." When Callie didn't say anything else, Dillon seemed to grow nervous. "Callie, if this isn't good for you, or you don't want to go, please tell me. You don't *have* to go."

"No, no, it's not that. I want to." This time Callie lost the battle of her conscience.

"Callie, what is it?"

"It's nothing."

Dillon touched her chin, forcing her to look into her eyes. Her voice was soft and encouraging. "I don't believe you."

Callie couldn't resist those eyes and that voice. "How can I go on a wonderful trip like this when my brother's in prison for murder because of me?"

After Michael went to Lompak, Callie found it difficult to live a normal life. Every morning she thought of him immediately. When she slept in on Sunday morning she felt guilty because he had to rise at six thirty whether he was ready or not. When she flipped through the one hundred and seventy-four channels out of boredom, she remembered that he could only watch what was showing in the rec room. When she debated about what to order at Subway, she recalled that his choices were to eat the meal in front of him or go hungry.

For the first few months she was consumed with guilt, barely able to go out of the house. Even a necessity like grocery shopping was almost too much for her. Ross had persuaded her—actually he dragged her to the car and drove her to see a psychologist. Finally, after her first dozen sessions, she began to believe the specialist in post-traumatic stress disorder who told her that her self-deprivation actually insulted Michael. He had risked his life to save hers and this was the way she thanked him? By withdrawing from life herself? After her second dozen treatments she stopped seeing the doctor and began to lead as normal a life as she could.

But going away with Dillon was different. Very different from doing what she needed to do to survive and be a productive member of society. She planned to spend time in the Bahamas purely for rest, relaxation, and pleasure. She would be taking a vacation from her life and didn't know if she was brave enough to do it.

❖

Dillon held her tolerant expression, even though she was tempted to walk Callie to the door and never come back. Callie was unlike any woman she'd met, and Dillon wanted to know more about her, even though she realized she shouldn't become even more involved than she already had. She rarely asked a woman a question that would make her open up like Callie just had. Typically she didn't care what was going on inside a woman's head, if anything, and it was always much less complicated to stay away from the touchy-feely aspects of her relationships.

But something in the way Callie was looking at her, a vulnerability that wasn't there before, made her want to ask even more such questions—and to stay. That and the fact that she needed her to clinch the deal with Bill. That thought disturbed her, so she pushed it to the back of her mind.

What had started out as an obligatory evening had turned into one she wasn't ready to end. "Why don't you invite me in, fix a pot of coffee, and tell me all about it?" Callie had already divulged the basic story the night they met, but Dillon knew there was more to it than that.

Callie searched Dillon's dark eyes, looking for what was behind her request. Other women with whom she shared the situation regarding Michael walked away and never returned. It was as though she were the murderer. No one could understand her situation and her devotion to her brother. No one would ever come between her and Michael, which was a death sentence for any relationship.

"If I tell you, you probably won't want me along." She doubted if Dillon remembered much about what she'd disclosed about Michael the night they had coffee after they danced at the bar.

"Why? Were you an accomplice and never got caught?" Dillon

had more experience with white-collar criminals than violent ones. This was way out of her league.

"Some people might think so."

"Let me be the judge of that. Come on, it's getting cold out here." Dillon slid out of the driver's seat and hurried around to the passenger door. She helped Callie from the car and didn't let go of her until Callie fumbled with her keys at the front door.

"Here, let me," Dillon offered. Callie's hand was shaking and the keys jingled when she handed them to Dillon. She grasped both the keys and Callie's fingers. "It's okay." She had no idea why she said that, and she didn't have a clue what was going on in Callie's life or if she even wanted any part of it. But Callie needed her right now and she needed Callie.

Coffee served, Callie sat in the overstuffed chair and put Dillon on the couch, separated by the narrow coffee table. Callie needed to regain distance from Dillon. She had never opened up this much so quickly to a woman. She was feeling the stress of money and Michael, and after tonight, surrounded by wealth and the kindness and generosity Phyllis bestowed upon her, she felt overwhelmed.

Dillon sat patiently across from her. "Why don't you start at the beginning?"

Callie took a deep breath, weighing her options. She was too far down the path to simply say forget it and ask Dillon to leave. Or was she? She could do that, but then she would never see her again. Even though Dillon might walk away, she had to tell her. She would either leave because of what she had to say or because she said nothing at all. But why was she here if she planned to simply go? She very easily could have said good night in the car and motioned for her to get out. But she didn't. She had taken her hand, made her meet her eyes, and asked. And ten minutes later she was still sitting in her living room waiting for her to speak.

All of these thoughts and a thousand more tumbled through Callie's brain like an avalanche. Not more than a minute went by before she made a decision that finally she could control.

"Michael is my younger brother, my only brother," she corrected herself, and the words started to flow and wouldn't stop if she'd wanted them to. Forty-five minutes later she sat back and took a deep, cleansing breath. Her hands were steady, her nerves calm, and her anticipation of what Dillon would say or do next hung over her head like a chandelier. She didn't have to wait long.

"Why do you think you're to blame for all of this?" Dillon was no shrink by any means, but even she knew Callie had taken on more responsibility for what happened that night and with Michael than she should.

"I don't feel responsible for being attacked," Callie shot back defensively.

Dillon remained calm and kept her voice even. "That's not what I said. I asked why you're assuming the blame. Those two men broke into *your* house. *They* attacked you and it was your brother who stopped them. Why does the responsibility for the actions of those men fall on your shoulders?"

Callie jumped out of the chair. "I don't feel responsible for the men who attacked me. They did it. They decided to try to kill me. Unlike what they did to me, no one had a gun to their head forcing them to do anything." Her body was flushed with heat and she was on the verge of a panic attack. She had reacted like this for months after the attack every time she thought about it. She took a few calming breaths.

"And why don't you say the same thing about Michael? From what you've told me, he's a grown man, capable of making his own decisions. You said it yourself several times, he's a wonderful, caring man. He made the choice because of who he is. Do you think he would have decided differently if someone else was in your shoes?"

Callie started to snap back at Dillon but stopped. Dillon wasn't judging her. She wasn't trying to tell her that what she was feeling was ridiculous, like most of the other people she had shared her story with. She was simply asking questions no one had ever asked before. Or if they had, the experience was still too raw in her mind for her to think clearly. Dillon was trying to understand her, not judge.

"No." The realization lifted a layer of guilt from her soul. "He would have done the same thing for a complete stranger on the street." She would always feel guilty that she was outside enjoying life and he was locked inside a cage. The guilt wasn't what drove her to fight for his freedom. She did so because she loved her brother, who had been wrongfully accused and convicted of actions he had no choice but to commit.

Dillon watched Callie struggle to control the emotions that danced across her face. She didn't hide her feelings well and seemed to have an even more difficult time when she was upset. First she had an almost empty stare, followed by a frown, then an expression that suggested acceptance. When Dillon thought Callie had regained her composure she asked, "So why are you hesitating about this weekend?"

Callie crossed the room but this time sat on the couch next to her. "I guess I just have a hard time enjoying myself, that's all," Callie said shyly.

She looked almost defeated, and however much Dillon wanted to stay, she knew it wasn't the smart thing to do. It would be difficult enough to distance herself from Callie after this weekend. She didn't need the added complication and ties of an emotional attachment thrown into the mix.

Dillon stood and pulled Callie to her feet. "As much as I hate to, I better go home. You've been through a lot tonight, and I don't want you to do something you might regret in the morning." She held Callie's hand as they walked to the front door, which creaked when she opened it. Standing on the threshold, she took both of Callie's hot hands in hers and imagined them on her body. She fought down her libido, which was yelling at her to step back inside. Instead, she kissed Callie on the cheek.

"I'll call you after I get the details from Bill." Dillon realized she had made the assumption, if not trapped Callie into coming with her to the Bahamas. But Dillon needed her this weekend. She felt a pang of conscience, but immediately pushed the unwelcome intruder out of her mind. Like her brother, Callie was a big girl, capable of making her own decisions.

CHAPTER EIGHT

Y ou're going where?"
"Paradise Island. It's in the Bahamas."
"I know where Paradise Island is, Callie. I just can't believe you're actually going, and with Dillon Matthews, of all people."

Callie tossed a hand towel at her best friend. "Come on, Audrey, what's the big deal? We were invited by one of Dillon's business associates."

Audrey finished clearing the dishes from the table. She rinsed the spaghetti sauce off their plates and set them in the sink. "The big deal is that you haven't been out on a date in God knows how long, and now you're going away for the weekend? Don't you think that's a little fast even for you?"

"Even for me?" Callie replied sarcastically. "Gee, thanks, Audrey, you make me sound like I jump into bed with every woman I meet."

After carrying their wineglasses into the living room, she settled on the couch. She wasn't angry at Audrey. They had been friends for over fifteen years and knew just about everything there was to know about each other. She'd been there when Audrey's mother died, and when Callie woke from her coma in the hospital, Audrey was the first person she saw.

"You know that's not what I meant. It's just that—shit, I don't know. Maybe I'm just jealous." Audrey plopped down on the couch next to Callie. "I mean, you meet Dillon Matthews at the bar while waiting for me. Jeez, maybe if I'd been there on time I'd be the one going to the Bahamas with the hottest woman on the planet."

Callie playfully elbowed her in the side. Despite the nagging guilt about enjoying herself, she was beginning to get excited about the trip. "See, I told you that you'd miss out on the biggest thing in your life someday because you can't get anywhere on time. And would you please stop saying *Dillon Matthews* as if her name would stop traffic."

"For Pete's sake, Cal, you still don't have any idea who she is, do you?"

An uncomfortable feeling was gnawing her gut. "Yes, Audrey, I do. She's successful, rich, and gorgeous. Big deal. She still puts her pants on one leg at a time. And speaking of putting on and taking off pants, I'm sure we'll have separate rooms. God only knows how many bedrooms were in the Franklins' house. I'm sure their place in Paradise Island has more than just two."

❖

Callie had never been more wrong.

"Here you are, ladies," Phyllis said happily. "There should be plenty of room for your clothes in the closet over here, and the bathroom is through that door." She pointed to the door on the other side of the small room that Callie estimated was five or six steps from where she stood rooted to the floor.

When they had arrived at the house, she knew it was smaller than the one where they attended the party, but she had no idea how much smaller. As Phyllis gave them the grand tour, Callie kept waiting to turn the corner and reach an additional wing containing all the bedrooms. They took several turns, and the final one ended in this small room that she was expected to share with Dillon. She didn't fault Phyllis. She had assumed they were a couple, and even if they weren't, the house still had only two bedrooms.

"I'll let you two get settled. Come into the kitchen any time. We usually have a cocktail on the patio and watch the sun set before dinner. You're welcome to join us."

"Thank you, Phyllis. We won't be long."

Callie was thankful Dillon said something because all she could focus on was the queen-size bed looming in the middle of the room, and all she could think about was lying naked with Dillon as the warm breeze floated through the window.

"Well." Dillon didn't know what else to say. It was obvious they both expected different sleeping arrangements, and any other time this would be an opportunity she wouldn't pass up. She had thought of Callie off and on for the past four days. Her smile, the smooth cadence of her voice, the feel of her skin under her lips... Rarely did a woman occupy her mind as much as Callie had. She was distracted at work, practically counting the days until they were together again.

Only on the flight over was she able to force herself to think of this weekend objectively. They were here together merely for business purposes, she told herself, and she would make sure nothing happened to disrupt her chances of getting Bill's land.

"Well," Callie repeated. "This is...unexpected." She actually wanted to say she felt as awkward as a teenager about to have sex for the first time.

"I'm sorry," Dillon said softly, and stepped farther into the room. Callie assumed she didn't want Phyllis to overhear their conversation any more than she did.

"There's nothing to be sorry about. It was a natural assumption, I guess. I mean, we did act like we were together." Callie cringed, knowing she was the one who had mostly acted that way that evening.

Dillon was in a quandary. She didn't know if she should tell Phyllis that she and Callie weren't lovers. What would she say? That this was their second date? How would that make her look? She knew she was being callous, but she was more afraid of what her confession would do to the deal than how it would affect her relationship with Callie or the Franklins.

"If I were the chivalrous type I'd volunteer to sleep in the chair, but since Phyllis has already labeled me a scoundrel, I'll take the left side," Dillon said, pointing to the bed. "We're adults. We can sleep in the same bed without becoming sexually involved." She was a very good liar.

Callie took her cue from Dillon and laid her suitcase on her side of the bed. "Of course we are. We're in a beautiful place with wonderful people with nothing but time on our hands for the next three days. We can get through this." Callie was a better liar.

She had spent the last three nights dreaming of Dillon. Monday night she was furious when Greg, not Dillon, phoned and informed her of their itinerary. She was pissed that Dillon couldn't find the time to call her herself. They were planning to spend the weekend together, for heaven's sake. Greg had been professional during their transactions, but she felt as if he were scheduling his boss to have sex. By the time Friday morning came around she had spoken to Greg more times than she had ever spoken to Dillon, and she was almost ready to cancel on principle. But when she saw Dillon on her front porch, all thoughts of principle went out the window.

Dillon was wearing a pair of khaki cargo shorts, a dark blue tank top that brought out the gray of her eyes, and a pair of well-worn flip-flops. Her legs were long and surprisingly firm for a person who sat behind a desk all day, or at least Callie thought she sat behind a desk all day. A small tattoo peeked out from the vicinity of her left breast, and Callie wanted to step closer to see what it was. Her left wrist bore a diver's watch, and a pair of Ray-Ban sunglasses dangled from the fingers of her right hand. She looked like she belonged on a beach. Her vague comment of going to Paradise Island a few times was pure bullshit.

Callie unpacked her suitcase while Dillon did the same. They passed several times on their way to the bathroom or the closet and once reached for the same drawer handle on the dresser. In short order, two toothbrushes were on the bathroom sink, two bottles of shampoo in the shower, and they went in search of their hosts.

Dillon had a difficult time putting one foot in front of the other. She couldn't help but see a lot of lace in the clothes Callie put in the drawers. Was it her normal clothing or had she bought something special for this trip, anticipating they would become intimate? Either way, Dillon had a hard time concentrating on anything other than a glimpse of the panty line on Callie's tight ass as she walked in front of her.

A warm blast of tropical air hit Dillon's face as they stepped out on to the patio. The sun was low in the sky, burning the horizon in shades of red and gold. The sunsets in the Bahamas were some of the most beautiful she had ever seen. Bill came forward, extending his hand.

"Welcome, Dillon and Callie. I'm sorry I wasn't able to meet you at the airport. A business crisis," he added, looking at Dillon knowingly. "But I promise that's the last time that topic will come up this weekend. We don't talk shop in this house. It's a promise I made to Phyllis early on in our marriage. I was working nonstop and we finally were able to get away for a few days. Phyllis made me swear I would never mention anything about the office here, and I've disappointed her only once."

What? Dillon was stunned. She expected to finalize the deal and had even carefully packed the papers in her suitcase. What in the hell was she going to do now? *Fuck.*

"It's been thirty years and the only time I broke that promise was right after the San Francisco earthquake back in 1989. I had a lot of property in the city." Bill stopped, obviously realizing he was beginning to do exactly what he said he wouldn't, and waved his hand as if to say, "Never mind." "Anyway, ladies, we're glad you could come down. Phyllis and I love this place. It's so peaceful and unspoiled by tourists and technology. It's where we reconnect with each other." Bill winked at Dillon.

Bill finally stopped talking long enough for Dillon to gather her wits and thank him again for inviting them to their home. Drinks were poured and Bill proposed a toast. "To three of the most intriguing women I know. May we all learn more about each other in the coming days that will draw us closer together." Phyllis clinked her glass first, with Dillon and Callie following.

"Your house is charming, Phyllis," Callie commented, settling in a chair to Dillon's right.

"We bought it when we didn't have two nickels to rub together. We scrimped and saved for years afterward and almost had to sell it once or twice, but somehow we got through. I know it's nothing compared to our house in Westwood, but this one suits us better. That one is more for show than anything else. Why in the world do we need seven bedrooms? It's only Bill and I. Our children are grown and scattered all over the country."

"How many children do you have?"

"Three, two boys and one girl," Phyllis replied to Callie's question. "All married to the same people they started out with, I'm proud to say. The divorce rate in this country is atrocious. Kids nowadays think it's easier to get out of a marriage than to get into one. 'Oops, we made a mistake,' they say. 'I don't love you anymore' and, poof, they're divorced. The sad thing is they don't think anything's wrong with that."

"How about grandchildren?" Callie expected Phyllis to start rattling off the names of her grandkids. What she didn't expect was the look of utter sadness that fell over both Phyllis and Bill's face. "I'm sorry, did I say something wrong?"

Bill was the first to speak up. He took Phyllis's hand. "No, of course not. We have six grandchildren. Five grandsons and one granddaughter. She passed away eighteen months ago."

Even though Callie had no way of knowing about this tragedy, she felt like an idiot. "I'm sorry for your loss." Their hosts tightened their grip on one another.

"Thank you. Haley was a junior at Tulane studying fine arts. She was a bright, wonderful, talented child. We always said she would be the next Picasso." Bill smiled as he described his granddaughter. "She was attacked outside her apartment by her neighbor when he realized she and Tammy were more than just roommates. He said he was called by God to save the institution of marriage. Haley and Tammy had been together for three years and were planning their wedding and had been profiled in the local newspaper. She died of her injuries three days after the attack."

Dillon laid her hand on Bill's arm. "I'm so sorry, Bill. I can't even imagine what you must have gone through, both of you," Dillon added, looking over at Phyllis. That explained a few things. No wonder he had been so insistent that she bring a date to the party and invited them both here to this house. He wanted them to know he approved of their lifestyle.

"Thank you, Dillon. It was a very difficult time for us. Haley had lived with us since she was seventeen. She and her mother didn't get along."

Phyllis interrupted angrily. "Didn't get along? When will you ever admit to yourself that Roxanne threw her own daughter out of the house? Our eldest son's wife," Phyllis added by way of explanation.

"Phyl, we don't need to talk about it now. We have guests." Bill clearly tried to distract his wife's attention, but it didn't work.

Phyllis turned to Dillon. "Do your parents know you're a lesbian?"

Dillon almost choked on her own saliva. No one had asked her that in more years than she could remember, and certainly not someone as old as Phyllis.

"Yes," Dillon replied cautiously. She and her mother never agreed on anything. In fact, her mother pretty much gave up on Dillon when she was in her early teens, but she and her father hadn't disowned her. Even though Dillon wasn't on the best of terms with them, she couldn't imagine what it must be like to be cast out like that.

Phyllis looked to Callie, who answered, "No." When Callie saw Dillon's head turn her way, she didn't make eye contact.

"May I ask why?"

"My father is long gone, and my mother and I have fallen out of touch." Callie hoped Phyllis wouldn't ask anything else. She didn't share her family history, or hysteria, as she called it, with people. Only her closest friends knew that her and Michael's childhood was filled with the drama of a mother who was manic-depressive, heavy on the manic, and a father who went to work one day and never came home. She and Michael began taking care of each other at a very early age.

"I'm sorry to hear that," Phyllis replied sympathetically. "I just don't understand how a mother could treat her own child like that."

Dillon could swear she heard a tsk, tsk in the comment

somewhere. "It sounds like Haley was lucky to have grandparents like you."

"We were the lucky ones," Bill said, resuming control of the conversation. "Now, enough of the melancholy. It's a beautiful Paradise Island evening and I insist we enjoy it."

They settled into the lounge chairs on the patio, the sun just starting to set over the horizon. Dillon's anger over the no-business edict had all but dissolved under the ugliness of the situation involving the Franklins' granddaughter. Before long she was joining the conversation as they talked about their plans for the next three days. Bill pointed to the dock, barely visible in the waning light, where they could rent Jet Skis or sign up for parasailing.

Dillon's body warmed at the thought of riding in front of Callie on a Jet Ski, Callie's arms around her waist as they bounced up and down in the clear water. Dillon got even warmer thinking about what Callie would look like in a bikini. She couldn't wait to find out. But first, she had to get through the night.

Chapter Nine

What had Dillon said? They were both adults and could sleep in the same bed without involving sex? Callie's body obviously did not get that memo. As soon as they started to climb the stairs, the butterflies in her stomach came alive and grew more agitated with each step. By the time she got to the top, she wasn't sure she could even stand up.

Phyllis and Bill had barbequed on the patio that evening and gave her and Dillon table-setting duty. They chatted easily throughout the meal but Callie sensed a guarded tension in Dillon. She didn't know her well at all, but the movement of her jaw muscles and her tight grip on her fork clearly signaled that she was nervous. Fortunately the Franklins didn't seem to notice anything amiss.

"You can use the bathroom first." The voice behind Callie startled her. She had been staring at the bed the minute she opened the door. It dominated the room, almost daring her to fill it with passion.

"Thanks." She opened the dresser drawer and pulled out her night clothes, then grabbed the bundle and headed for the bathroom. "I won't be long."

"Take your time," Dillon replied. "As a matter of fact, take all night," she added softly to the closed door that separated her from Callie. She practically fell onto the bed. She was a ball of nerves.

The flight, sitting next to Callie, their arms brushing against each other, their legs vying for the limited legroom, had initiated the torture. Then seeing the one bed, followed by the lace and straps of Callie's clothes, almost made her forget where she was and what type of business she actually intended to transact this weekend.

Dillon had never been as acutely aware of another woman in her life. She wondered why. Maybe because Callie was untouchable, or at least because she had decided to keep her hands off Callie. Maybe the way her voice sounded with the accompaniment of the waves in the background or the way she laughed at Bill's good-natured jokes. Maybe because she hadn't had sex in months. Whatever caused this reaction, she was stretched as tight as a drumhead, and if she wasn't careful, she would split. It would take only one word or touch from Callie or—

The bathroom door opened and Callie stood framed in the doorway, wearing pale blue women's boxer briefs and a matching blue tank top. The light was on, casting a warm silhouette around her. Dillon knew immediately that the lace around the trim of the pajamas was the lace she had glimpsed when they were unpacking.

Callie's legs were longer than she remembered, even though, like her, Callie had been in shorts all day. Her calves were perfectly formed, and her toenails were painted a medium shade of pink. Smooth shoulders held the thin straps, and Dillon's fingers tingled at the thought of what it would feel like to slide those straps slowly down Callie's arms. Firm, tight breasts with just a hint of erect nipple jutted out in the right places. Dillon hoped her mouth wasn't hanging open, but she didn't care if it was.

"It's all yours," Callie managed to say. The look on Dillon's face was enough to erase the doubt she felt a minute ago and replace it with something much more powerful.

When Callie had studied her reflection in the mirror behind the door, she wasn't sure if she was doing the right thing. She had brought two choices of sleepwear, this being the more provocative, and had grabbed it from the drawer without thinking. Other than that brief moment in the bar, Dillon hadn't indicated she was sexually interested in her. She wasn't sure what this weekend was all about. Was she here as Dillon's date and they would become lovers, or had they both been trapped into being here? The instant she had opened the door and saw Dillon's expression she knew what would happen.

Dillon didn't move, so Callie stepped into the room and dropped her clothes on the floor by her shoes, her back to Dillon. She felt rather than saw Dillon's eyes on her, and her body flushed with arousal, nipples hardening under the soft silk. She took a deep breath and turned around.

She was gone. Callie hadn't heard her move, but the sound of the shower water hitting the curtain told her where Dillon was. Half disappointed and half relieved, she finished getting ready for bed. As she crawled under the covers on her side of the mattress, she imagined the hot water sliding over Dillon's body not ten feet away.

Hot water wasn't sliding off Dillon's body, but cold. Ice cold. She had never understood why people took a cold shower to kill their arousal. It only made her teeth chatter. And it did practically nothing for the fire in her belly that raged now. She wanted to make love to Callie. Wanted to make love to her until neither of them could keep her eyes open. Then she wanted to do it again.

Callie's body was flawless, at least what she had seen, which was just about everything. Her choice of sleepwear left little to the imagination, and what Dillon did imagine drove her into the position she was in now. Her hands were on the wall in front of her, the water hitting the back of her head and cascading down her back like daggers. She tried closing her eyes, but every time she did, the image of Callie standing in the doorway cautiously offering herself flashed in her mind like a neon sign.

Dillon fought for control. She told herself over and over that sex with Callie Sheffield would only complicate the situation. She was here for just one thing—to get Bill to sign the papers. The goddamn papers that had to stay in her suitcase for at least the next three days. Shit, what was she going to do? How could she get through three days with Callie? More pressing, how could she get through tonight with Callie sleeping in the same bed and wearing nothing but blue lace?

Callie heard the water shut off. Dillon would soon join her. Should she be sitting up waiting for her? Should she pretend to be asleep? Would Dillon make the first move? Should she? What if Dillon wasn't interested? Sure, the look on her face telegraphed that she found Callie attractive, but that didn't mean Dillon wanted to have sex with her. Did it? Callie wasn't aggressive in bed and, if she admitted the truth to herself, she wasn't that confident either. None of the women she had been with ever complained, nor had they climbed out of bed and left, but none rocked her world either, and she seriously doubted she rocked theirs.

The sounds of movement stopped and Callie held her breath. Finally the door opened and Dillon stepped out wearing nothing but a towel. Her hair was wet and several drops of water clung stubbornly to a few end strands. Neither of them moved. The sound of the crashing waves intensified as the seconds passed, and the tension hung in the air. They seemed to be the only two people in the world.

Finally Dillon stepped forward. "I forgot my pajamas," she said, and lowered her head, feeling like a little girl. When Dillon had practically bolted into the bathroom she didn't stop long enough to grab her own nightclothes from the drawer. She had agonized over her dilemma for several minutes behind the closed door before finally gathering her courage to turn the knob. She felt silly. She had been naked in front of hundreds of women in every situation ranging from the locker room to countless other bedrooms. Why she was shy now troubled her. And here she was standing in the middle of the room in a towel. A very short towel.

Determined to keep her nervousness to herself, Dillon walked to the dresser and pulled out a pair of cotton boxer shorts. She cringed when she saw the airplanes all over them, but they were a gift from her sister. She couldn't backtrack so she lifted her chin and put first one foot, then the other into the unusual shorts. Then she pulled a soft, worn T-shirt over her head. *There. I did it. I managed to get dressed without embarrassing myself any more than I already have.*

With nothing else to do but hang up her towel and turn off the light, Dillon pulled back the covers on her side of the bed. She slid down, careful that her feet stayed on her side of the invisible dividing line and didn't wander into Callie's space and, worse yet, make contact with her. Mission accomplished, Dillon listened for the rhythmic cadence of Callie's breath.

"Sleep well." Callie's voice pierced the air.

Dillon knew Callie wasn't asleep, but the sound of her voice unsettled her anyway. "You too." She couldn't help but wonder if Callie had seen her less-than-beauty-pageant walk from the bathroom to the dresser. She was a sophisticated, successful woman. Why did she feel like a klutz? Less than a minute later she felt rather than heard Callie laugh.

"What is it?"

Callie burst into giggles. "Airplanes? I expected Calvin Klein, Hugo Boss, or Jockey, but not little airplanes on your underwear."

"A gift from my sister. She said I take myself way too seriously. That I need to loosen up." Dillon didn't know whether to be relieved or mortified. At least Callie's laughter had lessened the tension in the room.

"Do you? Take yourself too seriously, I mean, not loosen up, even though you fly around the world?" Callie rolled over on her back, breaking into another bout of giggling. The lights from the exterior landscaping were bleeding through the drapes, casting shadows across the ceiling.

"She seemed to think so, and to her that's all that matters."

"Do you have any other siblings?" Callie asked.

"Just my sister. I'm the oldest. Laura's the baby. Totally spoiled." After Dillon was born, her mom had three miscarriages before she finally had her sister, whom they gave practically everything from that point on. She was her dad's favorite and very quickly became the girly-girl daughter her mother didn't get in Dillon.

"Obviously she still is. I mean, she gave you those boxers, and the fact that you're wearing them only reaffirms the fact that she still gets what she wants." Callie giggled again.

"You weren't supposed to see them."

"Then why bring them?" Callie inhaled sharply, realizing her question implied that she would be seeing all of Dillon's underwear. Her face flushed and she was glad for the cover of darkness.

"All my underwear are funky."

Callie quickly rolled onto her side and propped her head in her hand. Dillon was on her back but it wasn't so dark that Callie couldn't see the expression on her face. "Funky?"

"I guess it's my anti-establishment statement. If I were a man I'd wear wild ties. I choose to wear crazy underwear. Some women like to wear thongs or satin or black lacy things from Frederick's of Hollywood. They think it makes them feel sexy. It's not for me to say otherwise."

"How does your underwear make you feel?"

Dillon turned on her side and steadily met her gaze, almost as if she admired her for asking such a bold question. Though, for an instant, Callie thought she might have gone too far.

"Like I've got a secret nobody knows about," Dillon said mischievously.

"Your secret is safe with me." When Dillon returned her smile Callie's stomach jumped into her throat. Her pulse was pounding in her ears. She cupped Dillon's face in her hand. The skin was cool but instantly turned warm on her palm. Dillon's eyes went from dark to almost pitch black as her pupils dilated even more. Her breathing hitched and desire flared in her eyes. Callie had to kiss her. The voice in the back of her head was screaming at her to kiss Dillon and kiss her now. She licked her lips and bent her head.

Dillon couldn't think and suddenly found it very difficult to breathe. As if in slow motion, Callie's lips took forever to close the gap between them. When Callie hesitated a millimeter away, Dillon thought she would die if Callie didn't kiss her. Warm breath caressed her lips, and finally the space that separated them disappeared. Dillon forgot the shock of being in such a submissive position when Callie expertly explored her lips. Her kisses were soft and tentative as she nibbled first on her top lip, then the bottom. By the time Callie fully tasted every inch, Dillon had wrapped her hands behind her neck and was pulling her closer.

Callie fought for control but wasn't really sure why she should restrain herself. It was a warm, tropical night, the wind gently blowing the half-open curtains. A sensuous woman was lying next to her in bed kissing her deeply. Wasn't this what movies were made of?

She didn't know when she had gone from kissing Dillon to being under her, but she didn't care. Dillon's weight was comforting, not smothering like that of other lovers she had been with. Dillon's hands roamed freely over her bare skin as she deepened the kiss. Callie wrapped her arms around Dillon's shoulders in encouragement. Insistent hands traveled up and down her legs, drawing Callie deeper into the sensations.

Callie wasn't about to be left out of the exploratory mission, so she eased her hands under Dillon's shirt. Hard, tight muscles contracted as her fingers glided over Dillon's womanly curves. She was on fire. Her body had been without the touch of a woman for so long, she was afraid she might spontaneously combust any moment. She felt alive for the first time in forever, and she didn't want the feeling to end. She wanted to dissolve in sheer pleasure, she needed to escape into passion, and Dillon was offering her that opportunity now. She found the waistband of Dillon's boxers and pulled them off. Unfortunately, as she tossed them over Dillon's head the vision of giant red, green, and yellow airplanes soaring in the air struck her as hysterically funny. She started laughing and couldn't stop.

At first, Dillon thought Callie was ticklish. She had been kissing and nibbling on her favorite place of a woman's neck when she started laughing. She moved a little to the left and the laughing continued. Finally the pressure of hands pushing her away permeated her lust-filled brain and she lifted her head. Callie was looking at her with alarm in her eyes, but the hand over her mouth stifling her giggles told her something different. Dillon had been with many women, but none of them had found humor in her lovemaking techniques. Callie must have sensed her confusion because she quickly spoke.

"No, Dillon, it's not you. I'm not laughing at you." Callie pulled her down for a series of kisses, trying, Dillon supposed, to assuage her doubt. "It's just that when your boxers…the airplanes…" Callie dissolved into another bout of near hysterics, covering her face with her hands.

Dillon rolled onto her back and threw her arm over her eyes. Never in her life had she encountered this response, and she had been involved in some pretty weird stuff between the sheets. "That was interesting. I'll have to tell Laura to buy plain white next time."

Callie started to snicker again and this time Dillon joined her. Then she commented dryly, "I guess the moment has passed." The passion that had consumed her was back under control, her mind grateful for the interruption. She was not going to have sex with Callie. No, she was going to sleep with her, just not *sleep* with her. Already she was confused.

Callie was afraid she had insulted or humiliated Dillon, but she couldn't help herself. She must have cracked under the stress of her life. But here? Now? If it weren't so absurd it would be horrific. They started to giggle again and both tried to get the other to stop, trading "shh's" and "stops" back and forth, which only caused more hooting and chuckling until finally the room grew quiet. They both lay on their backs, chests heaving from the exertion.

Feeling as though a weight had been lifted off her shoulders, Callie told herself that Dillon wanted her, no doubt about it. But she was right, the moment had passed. Callie was sure that if either of them even looked at the other, they would both be naked in a heartbeat, picking up where they left off. And this time they wouldn't stop. For some reason, either side of that equation didn't bother her. If Dillon made a move she wouldn't stop her, but if she didn't, she would sleep soundly, knowing Dillon was beside her. "I guess you're right about that moment we lost. I'm sorry. I just couldn't get the image out of my mind." She fought down the tingle of laughter building inside her.

"Please, stop apologizing. It's okay. I guess if the underwear were on the other foot, so to speak, I'd probably do the same thing. But I'm still going to speak to Laura."

Callie was overwhelmingly relieved at Dillon's sense of humor. She had been horrified at her loss of control and knew she would be lucky if Dillon didn't put her on the next flight out of here. She couldn't help one last jab. "I can't wait to see what you're wearing tomorrow."

"Good night, Callie," Dillon said sternly, with a trace of humor in her inflection.

"Good night, Captain." Callie drifted off to sleep, smiling.

Chapter Ten

D illon's underwear of the day would have to wait because she was asleep when Callie woke. Carefully she lifted the sheet and peeked at Dillon's naked body. Sometime during the night Dillon had discarded her T-shirt, which lay on the floor near her boxers. She was on her side, offering Callie a perfect view of her smooth, round ass. The distinct tan line at her waist showed that Dillon wasn't totally bound behind her desk. Callie's fingers itched to trace the smooth lines of her back, cross the rise of her hip, and disappear into the vee between her legs.

She wanted to wake Dillon with her fingers, her mouth, and her body, to lightly skim over the soft skin and feel Dillon's muscles respond. She yearned to explore every inch of her and then do it again and again. She needed to either act on her desires or get out of bed now. A subtle cough from the next room quenched any further thought of morning entertainment. Callie certainly didn't fancy the Franklins overhearing their lovemaking.

After watching Dillon for a few more minutes, she got up and went downstairs in search of the coffeepot. Bill was already sitting on the patio. "May I join you?"

"Of course you may. Please sit." Bill motioned to a chair to his right. "I see you found the coffee," he said, indicating the steaming cup that Callie grasped.

"Yes, thank you. I can't function in the morning anymore without it. I'm not sure if it's a bad habit or an addiction. Either way, I'm a grouch until I've had my first cup." Callie leaned back in the lounge chair and put her feet up. It was early and the breeze blowing in from the ocean was still cool. The sun was warm on her face and the sky was cloudless. Bill respected her first-cup grouchiness and didn't say a word. There was no need to fill the silence with conversation.

"Can I get you a refill?" Bill was looking at her expectantly.

"You don't have to do that. I can do it myself." She swung her legs off the chair to stand up.

"Nonsense, I'm getting some anyway. You stay put. I'll be back in a jiffy." He took her cup and disappeared into the house.

Jiffy? Callie couldn't remember anyone using the word "jiffy" in ages. The Franklins were truly unpretentious.

She had enjoyed dinner last night. Bill and Phyllis were younger in heart and opinions than most people half their age. Not that she knew many older people, but those she did certainly didn't act like the Franklins. The way they talked and asked questions about her childhood and family made her feel comfortable and at home. When she stumbled over a question that could have involved a discussion of Michael, they seemed to understand her hesitation and quickly moved on to another topic. Several times during the evening she wondered what her life would have been like if Bill and Phyllis had been her parents.

"I love it out here in the morning," Bill said, setting her cup on the coaster. "I could sit here all day. As a matter of fact, some days that's exactly what I do."

"I can understand that. It's beautiful." Callie couldn't remember the last time she'd been so relaxed. She had been here less than twenty-four hours, but she felt as if she'd always lived here. The sun was casting shadows on the beach, and she was surprised when she wished she had brought her paints with her. She hadn't picked up a brush since the attack.

"I hope you slept well," Bill said.

Callie thought she detected an element of teasing in his question and flushed as she remembered the passion and giggling of the night before. The house was small. Just how much had he and Phyllis heard? Anyone listening to the sounds emanating from their bedroom could very well have mistaken them for pillow talk and lovemaking.

"Very well, thank you," was all she could manage to say. She tried to see Bill's face out of the corner of her eye but it was angled away.

"Dillon is an interesting individual."

Bill's statement was more of an opening for conversation about Dillon than an observation. Callie trod carefully. "Yes, she is."

"She's too intense, a classic Type A. Workaholic, driven to success, always on the go, even when she's asleep. She needs to learn to relax. Life will pass by her without her knowing when it happened."

This time Callie did turn to look at Bill. It sounded like he was speaking about himself, and she asked him if it was so.

"Yes. I was too busy when my kids were growing up. I can barely remember going to one of my sons' baseball or football games. Haley's mom was the homecoming queen and I was in Europe that night. I missed a lot of their formative years. I thank God every day for Phyllis. She's the glue that held our family together. Still does, as a matter of fact. I don't know where I'd be without her. Actually I do know where I'd be—slinging hash at the VA hospital without a dime to my name and a dozen kids scattered around the country."

Callie laughed at his description. "I bet you had something to do with all of this." Callie waved her hands around her.

"Nah, I just wrote the check. Phyllis is the one that cashed it." Bill sipped his coffee for a few minutes before he continued. "I see a lot of me in Dillon."

"Really? Phyllis said the same thing at the dinner party. Called her a scoundrel." Callie thought this a good way to learn more about her weekend date.

Bill laughed. "Did she now? She used to call me that before I settled down and we got married. Then Dillon's definitely a lot like I was when I was younger. She's strong, impulsive, cautiously reckless, and very successful."

"You seem to have done your research." The items Bill listed were certainly more than she could say about her roommate.

"I'm a businessman. I know about the people I'm dealing with."

Callie detected a sense of sadness in his voice. "And do you like what you see in Dillon?"

Bill turned in his chair and met her look head-on. "I'm not sure yet."

Callie was surprised at the honesty of Bill's confession. He had to know she would repeat his opinion to Dillon. He was either very wise or very careless. She doubted it was the latter.

"Not sure about what, dear?" Phyllis's strong voice entered the conversation.

If Bill gave any indication he was upset by his wife's eavesdropping, Callie didn't pick up on it. But she did see his face light up, and he rose from the chair to kiss Phyllis on the cheek.

"Not sure if you had any plans for today? I imagine Callie and Dillon would like some time alone to explore the island. Callie, just because we invited you and Dillon down here doesn't mean you're obligated to spend the entire weekend with us. We're just a couple of old folks."

"Speak for yourself, Bill." Phyllis playfully slapped her husband's arm. "I'll have to remind you that I am seven months younger than you. A fuddy-duddy I am not, and don't you forget it."

Fuddy-duddy? Now Callie was certain she had fallen back in time. These two were the most pleasant people she had met in a long time. She hoped that when she was their age, she would still be this energetic and feisty. A tingle down her neck told her that Dillon was standing behind her.

"Good morning, Dillon. I hope you slept well. Come, please sit down. Would you like some coffee?" Phyllis rattled off, ever the hostess.

"Good morning to you too and, yes, I did sleep well, and some coffee would be great." Dillon didn't join them but walked over to the banister and looked out at the ocean.

Callie studied Dillon as she casually leaned against the rail. Her hair was wet and she wore a pair of navy surfer shorts trimmed in white piping, which hung off her hips like she had been born in them. Her tank top covered a sports bra the same shade of blue as her shorts. A tattoo of turtles crawled up the outside of her right calf above bare feet.

"All this sunshine and fresh air is going to kill me." Dillon squinted against the bright morning rays of the sun. She wasn't much of a morning person except for when she woke up with the right woman, and she wasn't surprised this morning that she woke up alone. She debated about turning around to face Callie, but instead took a moment to recall the fire in her veins at their first kiss. Soon she was almost as aroused as she was last night, but she put a damper on her lust and directed her attention to her hosts instead.

"I want to thank you again for inviting us, Bill." She nodded her gratitude to Phyllis for the cup she placed in her hand.

"It's my pleasure, Dillon. I don't mean to be presumptuous, but indulge an old man. You looked like you were under a lot of stress and needed to relax."

Dillon's radar went up, trying to detect if he meant their deal or just life in general. "I'm pretty much always like this. My assistant Greg keeps scheduling me for vacations and always has to cancel at the last minute. I think he gave up sometime last year."

Bill laughed. "Now, Dillon, don't give up on yourself. You'll find something or someone to make you want to settle down. And when you do, it won't even be difficult. You'll wonder why you didn't do it sooner."

Dillon was glad for her sunglasses. She glanced at Callie when Bill mentioned a "someone." She had considered spending more time on her personal life, but every time she thought she had reached a point in her career to do it, something better came along. Another piece of land, another project, another client.

Callie wouldn't meet her eyes, and Dillon didn't know if it was because of Bill's comment or last night. Callie was absolutely adorable. She was hot, passionate, and a fabulous kisser. But she was also a lot of fun. That thing with her underwear was something Dillon would probably never forget. She realized Bill was looking at her for a response.

"I'm afraid that's not going to happen, Bill." Dillon hesitated, seeing the shocked expression on his face and in Callie's eyes. She hid a grin behind her coffee cup. "Phyllis is already taken."

All four broke out in laughter and were still chuckling when Phyllis added, "Don't worry, Dillon. I've been giving your girl Callie pointers."

The laughter died down. "Thank you, Phyllis, but Callie is doing just fine on her own." She slid the Ray-Bans down her nose, locking eyes with a blushing Callie.

"Yes, we heard," Phyllis added softly.

"Oh, God." Callie looked like she wanted to curl up and die. What was Dillon supposed to say to that? If she denied that anything had happened, she would look childish, and if she said nothing… well. Well, something did happen last night. Something other than the giggles over airplanes. Callie had responded to caresses, ignited under her fingertips. Dillon had wanted her then and she wanted her now.

"I have to apologize for that. I said something stupid and Callie got the giggles. And once she starts, it's hard for her to stop. She just has to get it all out and then she's fine. I'm sorry if we disturbed you." Dillon never took her eyes off Callie, who had buried her face in her hands.

"Think nothing of it, Callie. It's good to hear the sound of love in the house again." Bill squeezed his wife's hand.

Love? Dillon no longer heard the waves crashing on the shoreline. The world disappeared except for Callie, who looked as shocked as Dillon felt.

Love? We've just met, for God's sake.

❖

Breakfast over, Dillon suggested a walk on the beach and caught a knowing glance between their hosts. Both Bill and Phyllis suddenly had something to do, leaving Callie to accompany her. The sand was soft under her feet and slid easily between her toes. Scattered along the shoreline were sunbathers, sun worshipers, and day-after sunburns. Several kids were building a sand castle while a wave chased a giggling toddler back to his mother.

Dillon tried to relax. She wasn't comfortable with free time. She couldn't remember when she had absolutely nothing to do. For years her days were planned out for her whether they included meetings, site visits, or investors. Work was her life, and when she wasn't working, she was thinking about it. Right now she was thinking about what was on her desk when she left yesterday and what would be waiting for her when she returned.

But mostly she was mulling over what was not going to be on her desk Tuesday morning. Bill Franklin's signature on a deed of sale. She had negotiated for hundreds of acres with less trouble than Bill was giving her now. What did he want? What did he really want from her? Obviously it wasn't money; he had plenty of his own. What had Greg said? He wanted to see if there was something behind her business persona. Why in the hell did he care who she was? And what business of his was it anyway? Dillon shook her head, trying to get the pieces to fall into place. What in God's name did she have to do for four stupid acres?

Callie matched her step for step. Occasionally she stopped and picked up a shell or scampered out of the way of an aggressive wave sweeping too far in. She hadn't tried to engage Dillon in conversation, but walked quietly beside her. Callie was an interesting dichotomy. On the one hand she was shy and naïve, and on the other she had a level of sophistication Dillon didn't expect.

From what she had gathered so far, Callie had spent her childhood on the lower end of middle class, and she was working toward a better life when her plans were derailed. She was totally unselfish when it came to her brother and clearly wouldn't rest until he was free. She was kind, thoughtful, supportive, and self-confident. And she was attractive in a sensuous, subtle way. In some respects she was everything anyone could want in a wife.

Dillon stopped. Callie took several steps before she also stopped and glanced back with a question in her eyes. *That's it! That's what I have to do.* The realization of exactly how she would prove to Bill that she was worthy, or whatever he wanted from her before he sold her his land, was right before her eyes. It had been there all along, she just couldn't see it. She hadn't been looking for it, and if it was a wall, she would have walked right into it, bounced off, and kept going.

An overwhelming, almost oppressive cloud lifted from around her. She wouldn't let Bill continue to string her along while she waited helplessly for him to give his approval. She hated not being in charge and she intended to end this situation today. Right here, right now. Everything she needed to clench this deal stood five feet in front of her. *Callie*.

CHAPTER ELEVEN

D illon, are you all right?" Callie asked. Dillon hadn't said a word or broken stride since they hit the beach twenty minutes ago. She seemed to be lost in her own thoughts, and Callie didn't want to disturb her.

"I'm fine, now," Dillon said. "I'm glad you were able to come." She resumed her pace, this time walking near Callie.

Callie sensed a change in Dillon that she attributed to the sun, the sand, and the surf. "I'm glad I could too. Thank you for asking me." She walked a few more steps before she posed the question that had been dancing on her lips for several days. "Why did you ask me? I mean, it's kind of risky to invite someone you barely know to go away for the weekend. And this is *really* away." The four hours on the plane was longer than she spent on her last date eons ago.

"You're interesting and appear to be able to enjoy yourself without having to be entertained. You hit it off fabulously with Phyllis and she likes you." Dillon removed her sunglasses and her eyes trailed a lazy path from head to toe, then slid back. "And I can think of worse things to look at for four days." Dillon punctuated her reply by kicking water on Callie's legs.

Dillon's visual caress of her body sent such strong shock waves through Callie that she suddenly felt uncomfortable and needed some distance. "Last one to the pier has to buy the drinks." She took off running in the direction they were headed.

Dillon was left flat-footed by the quick change of mood, and Callie was at least ten yards ahead of her before her body caught up with her brain. She ripped off her flip-flops and chased her. Callie turned around and did a little you-can't-catch-me dance, and when she did she tripped and tumbled several times before coming to a stop on her back. Dillon was standing over her in an instant.

"Aha. That's what you get when you act cocky." Dillon's breath caught in her throat. Callie's chest was heaving from the exertion and the smile filling her face was breathtaking. Their positions in the sand reminded Dillon of the classic beach scene in *From Here to Eternity* when Burt Lancaster stood over Deborah Kerr. The waves were crashing around them when Burt's character, Sergeant Milton Warden, dropped to his knees and took Karen Holmes in his arms and kissed her. The scene played in Dillon's head until she could do nothing other than mimic the most powerful love scene of all time.

When their lips met, Callie responded instantly, and she wrapped her arms around Dillon's neck. Dillon kissed her with so much skill and passion that she knew she had made Callie forget about everything. The water lapped around them and Callie didn't indicate that she even noticed.

But Dillon did notice and her brain kicked in. As much as she wanted to continue kissing Callie, people were everywhere. It was still early and the beach wasn't nearly as full as it would be in a few hours, but they still had to be careful. Against her will and definitely against her body's protests, Dillon pulled back from Callie's hot lips.

"I don't think we should do this here." Dillon had told herself earlier that it wasn't in her best interest to have sex with Callie, but her recently formulated action plan changed all that. It was in her best interest not only to have sex with Callie this weekend, but to get her to fall in love with her. If that's what Bill wanted to see, that's what she'd give him.

Dillon's voice was husky and Callie wanted to drown in it. She searched her face for any sign of rejection, but Dillon's sunglasses hid her eyes. Callie wasn't so far out of practice not to recognize when she was being kissed back, passionately. And then there was last night. If not for her stupid case of the giggles, they would have made love.

"What do you think we *should* do?" Dillon was still lying almost on top of her, their breasts touching through their now-wet clothes. Dillon's body was hot, their legs intertwined. The flash of desire in Dillon's eyes told Callie exactly what she wanted to do. Callie knew her eyes said the same thing.

"I suppose it would be rude to go back to the house and lock ourselves in the bedroom for the rest of the trip," Dillon answered, with a charm and seductive gaze that Callie found much harder to resist than outright directness.

Callie had just started breathing normally again, but she almost panted when Dillon implied they would make love for the next four days. Now, there was a thought. Dillon's lips were teasing her with their closeness, and she had to fight to keep from covering them once more. "At times like these I hate my mother for instilling good manners in me." It was the only good thing she had done for her. Callie pushed against Dillon's chest while she still had the strength. Dillon rolled off and pulled her up in one motion. "Okay, now where were we?" she asked, trying to regain some sense of control.

"I think we were racing to the pier," Dillon answered, brushing the sand off her butt and legs. She even reached into her sports bra to brush off sand that had slipped inside. Callie watched every move and Dillon's nipples tightened under her gaze. When Callie licked her lips, Dillon stopped. Callie couldn't respond. "On second thought, I've got a better idea," Dillon said. "Ever been on a Jet Ski?"

❖

The water was cold, but Callie was shielded from most of the drenching by Dillon's body in front of her. She was a good swimmer but had never been on a Jet Ski and opted to sit behind Dillon until she got the hang of how to handle the machine. When she first climbed on she was nervous but after a few minutes began to relax, and before she knew it, she was grateful for her place behind Dillon. She had to hang on so as not to be tossed off, which provided her the perfect opportunity to wrap her arms around Dillon's strong body.

Their bulky life vests prohibited any direct body contact, but she could touch Dillon's arms whenever she wanted. She wanted to but stopped herself.

She wasn't even in the same league as Dillon. Dillon was successful, sophisticated, shockingly good-looking, and horribly rich. She, on the other hand, barely had a pot to piss in, as her father used to say. At least when he was still around, he used to say it. Callie remembered a few things about her father, and they were usually smart-ass remarks like that one.

"Wanna take a turn?" Dillon asked, backing off the throttle. The craft bobbed up and down in the water, the rhythm seductive. Callie was spooned behind Dillon, who turned around and laid her hand on Callie's leg. Dillon's hand was slick from the salt water, and Callie's leg tensed involuntarily under Dillon's fingers as she caressed it gently, stroking up and down Callie's thigh.

Callie's stomach turned, and it wasn't because of the rocking of the ocean. Dillon's wandering fingers on her leg crept higher with each stroke, and Callie watched each move. Only when they stopped moving did Callie lift her head and meet hot, mischievous eyes. A drop of water snaked its way down Dillon's forehead in the direction of her left eye, and Callie's own hand shook when she reached up and intercepted it. Dillon caught her wrist and kissed her palm before she had a chance to stop the bead from dissolving into her eyebrow.

Dillon's eyes never left hers as she first kissed, then seductively licked her palm. Flames shot up her arm, through her stomach, and landed squarely between her legs. What Dillon was doing tickled but was the most sensuous thing she had ever experienced. Dillon pulled her forward, and just before their lips met, the weight of both of them on one side of the Jet Ski was too much. They both toppled off into the water.

Dillon surfaced first, with Callie not far behind. "Shit, that water's cold." It was still early in the summer season, and even though the outside temperature was warm, the water was much colder.

"Are you all right?" Dillon asked, concerned. Callie had said she could swim, but the unexpected dump could be disorienting.

"I'm fine." Callie laughed and glanced toward the Jet Ski, floating aimlessly nearby as if waiting for the next rider to buck off. "How do we get back on?"

Dillon laughed in relief. "Now that's the tricky part."

And tricky it was. After several attempts, most of which had them ending up back in the water, they were back on board, this time with Callie in the driver's seat. She quickly acclimated to the throttle, and they were soon jumping waves and perfecting rooster tails under the midday sun.

Dillon took full advantage of sitting behind Callie. She wasn't nearly as shy about caressing Callie's arms and even let her hands wander over as much of her thighs as she could reach. Callie's driving turned erratic when Dillon's hands were anywhere other than clasped around the life vest turned chastity belt. She didn't doubt that Callie was attracted to her, but was thrilled nonetheless.

With the help of Dillon's outstretched hand, Callie climbed off the Jet Ski, careful not to spill again. The dock was crowded now with other people wanting a turn on the fast machines. Dillon turned over the key to the attendant with one hand and kept her grip on Callie's with the other. They chatted about their water adventure and then nothing in particular as they walked along the shoreline back to the house, holding hands the entire way.

Phyllis was sitting on the patio reading a Harlequin romance. Dillon recognized the cover as one of the kind of paperbacks that filled several shelves in her sister Laura's study. She used to tease Laura that it was totally uncool for a patent attorney to read romance novels. Once Laura was so frustrated at Dillon's jibes that she shot back, "At least someone's getting sex, because it certainly isn't me." They laughed about that remark the morning of Laura's wedding to her husband Tim. A fleeting thought about Phyllis and Bill's sex life flashed through her mind, and she just let it keep moving.

"You two have a good time?"

"Yes, we did. Except for the water being a little cold, it was absolutely beautiful. It's so clear you can see all the way to the bottom. The color is amazing and the—" Callie stopped in mid-sentence and laughed. "I guess I don't need to tell you any of this, do I, Phyllis?"

"No, but it's always fun to hear about someone's first time down here."

Dillon didn't hear anything else Phyllis said, preferring to plan her and Callie's first time down here, as she called it. This wasn't her first time anywhere. She had been to the Bahamas many times, seduced dozens of women, and closed hundreds of deals. She knew what she needed to do, and she would have Callie and a signed deed by the end of tomorrow.

Dinner over, Dillon could hardly wait to be alone with Callie. She was attracted to her, but she also needed to lock her in, at least until the papers were signed. She had flirted with and teased Callie all afternoon and well into the evening, and much to her delight, Bill and Phyllis joined in. Bill was seeing what he wanted to, and Callie was playing her part flawlessly, even though she didn't realize it.

Dillon's scheme was working, and even though sleeping with Callie was part of the plan, it certainly wasn't another day at the office. Finally it was late enough for them to say good night without being overly rude and dashing toward the bedroom. But who was she fooling? Bill's deep laughter followed them up the stairs.

Callie stiffened when she heard the door lock. The sound echoed in the small room. It signaled loud and clear what was about to happen. And she knew it would. She wanted it to. Nothing would or could stop them from consummating their attraction tonight. And she was scared shitless.

She had her share of sexual experiences, but not lately, and certainly not with a woman of Dillon's caliber.

Dillon must have read her mind because she said, "It's just you and me here, Callie. I don't want to speak for you, but I think it's safe to say you're attracted to me."

Callie's chuckle came out more calm than she felt. "Ya think?"

Dillon smiled. "I'm attracted to you. We're in a beautiful place, with good people, the sun, and now the stars. What more do we need?" Dillon slowly approached Callie, who momentarily felt like turning and running. She took Callie's hand and kissed the same palm she'd kissed earlier that morning in the middle of the bay.

Dillon's kiss caused the same reaction this time as the one earlier, so she kissed Dillon's hand in return. She could even taste a trace of salt on her skin left behind by the sea water from this morning. Her stomach jumped and she found it difficult to breathe. "I think I need my head examined." Callie tried to dispel her nervousness with laughter.

"Why is that?"

"Because even though I know we really shouldn't do this, I'm going to anyway." Callie stepped forward and held Dillon's face in her hands. She caressed Dillon's cheeks and lips with her thumbs. She looked into gray eyes that turned black under her gaze. Her heart was racing so loud she couldn't have heard herself think if she had to. So she didn't. She kissed Dillon instead.

Callie always thought the descriptor of rockets exploding behind your eyes was a myth created by the authors of those trashy romance novels Phyllis was reading this afternoon. But when her tongue disappeared inside Dillon's mouth, she took back everything she had ever said about them. Every nerve in her body came alive, and she thought she would explode from the sensations that threatened to overwhelm her.

Dillon's tongue darted in and out of her mouth while her hands roamed freely over her body. One by one Dillon opened the buttons on her shirt and replaced the cool breeze on her skin with her hot hands. Alternatively caressing then demanding, her fingers explored Callie's stomach and back, inching tantalizingly closer to her breasts with each stroke. When Dillon's palm cupped her breast she inhaled sharply and pulled Dillon closer. Dillon released her mouth and turned her attention to the valley between her breasts.

With agonizing slowness Dillon unhooked her bra, and her breasts spilled out into her waiting hands. Dillon's thumbs gently caressed her nipples, which grew harder under the attention. Dillon's lips were hot on her flesh and she squeezed her breasts together and kissed them both. Suddenly Callie pushed her away. "Take your clothes off. I want to feel you. I need your skin on mine."

Dillon gazed into her eyes and kissed her again, this time softly and tenderly. Callie lay on the bed and watched Dillon shrug out of her shirt and step out of her shorts, her boxers ending in a heap at her feet. Today's underwear was adorned with rowboats, and Callie thanked God she didn't have a repeat of the giggles. Dillon gazed down at her, pulling off her shorts and panties, and Callie watched as she revealed inch after inch of her flesh. The edges of the tattoo she saw yesterday led to a vivid image of a phoenix rising from its own ashes, which began just above her left nipple. Why would Dillon choose such an unusual bird for a tattoo? But the question faded when Dillon licked her lips. Callie thought she might climax from Dillon's simple action. She reached up and pulled her down on top of her.

"God, you feel good," Callie said as she wrapped her arms and legs around Dillon's hard body. Dillon murmured something into her neck as she slid her thigh between Callie's legs. Callie arched toward the pressure, eager for release.

"Shh, not yet," Dillon answered her thrusts. "We have all night and I'm not ready for you to let go. I want to see you, touch you, taste every inch of you." And she did.

They made love for hours, sucking, tasting, nibbling, demanding, coaxing, and worshiping each other's bodies. Callie had never been so loved and explored, and when Dillon entered her for the first time, she had never felt so full. Dillon was gentle, yet she demanded more from Callie than she had ever given. Dillon's tongue was like feathery magic on her clitoris, and her fingers unerringly found the most sensitive spots on her body. They were covered in sweat and sex, arms and legs intertwined when Callie finally fell asleep, exhausted.

CHAPTER TWELVE

Hair tickled Dillon's nose. She was lying on her back with Callie curled into her side. One arm was across her stomach, and Dillon stroked the leg that lay seductively across the top of her thighs. Callie had been asleep for an hour, or at least Dillon thought it was an hour. She had listened to the deep rhythmic cadence of her breath as it slowed. Dillon was too wired to drift off, the effects of their lovemaking lasting long after her last climax. This was unusual for her. She either fell dead to the world or calmly got out of bed and went home. Rarely did she go in for snuggling or the current intimacy.

Callie had been a dynamic lover. Once she got over her initial shyness, she was active, eager, and insatiable. Dillon smiled against the warm head lying on her chest. Actually, she couldn't remember anyone driving her as crazy as Callie had last night. She couldn't keep her hands off her, and every time Dillon tried to take control, Callie pushed her away until she was ready for her.

If sex with Callie was the reward for an added complication of Bill's land, Dillon had no complaints and no regrets, especially if it was fabulous sex. Dillon frowned. Had she prostituted herself for this business arrangement?

No, of course not. She was hot for Callie and Callie was a willing participant. Didn't that make them two consenting adults? Callie was aware that Dillon wanted Bill's land. She'd known that when they went to dinner. Dillon had made it clear she needed a date for the dinner party and why. How much more obvious could she be?

Dillon lay quietly, still unable to sleep. Her brain jumped at lightning speed from one topic to the other, the ties between them threadbare yet connected. She wished she were one of those women who after making love could simply relax and enjoy the afterglow, let her mind wander, think of absolutely nothing. But here she was with a beautiful woman in her arms, thinking about land permits, construction delays, and the price of concrete.

Callie rolled over onto her side and pulled Dillon with her. Her blond hair smelled like strawberries, and Dillon buried her face deep in the back of her neck. Callie's head was cradled in the crook of one of her arms while her other one was free to roam the body pressed tight against her chest. Callie's legs were long and the gentle swell of her hip enticing. Dillon moved her hand back and forth, paying special attention to the hills and valleys that made up the breathtaking landscape of Callie's body. With each stroke, she desired Callie more, but for the first time ever she was content to caress solely for pleasure instead of arousal.

Callie was still sleeping soundly when Dillon finally got up. She wanted to stay in that same position forever, but she finally had to give in to the thousand needles pricking her arm on which Callie lay. The dresser drawer creaked when she tried it and she froze, turning around to see if Callie had awakened. She didn't move, and Dillon slowly opened the drawer just enough to slide out a pair of shorts and a T-shirt. She pulled on a robe over her clothes and silently closed the bedroom door behind her.

When Dillon entered the room Phyllis was standing next to the coffeepot, pouring a cup. She gave Dillon the once-over and held out her hand. "It looks like you need this more than I do."

Dillon had some idea of how she looked, since she had barely slept all night. "Thanks." She cradled the cup, inhaling the rich aroma. She felt better already. Just as she was about to take her first sip, a hand passed over her shoulders and down her arm in a touch only lovers share.

Callie sat down beside her and she said, "I thought you were asleep."

Dillon's stomach jumped a little when Callie looked deep into her eyes. Morning-after shy she was not. "I was, but when I woke up you were gone." Callie's voice was quiet, so only Dillon could hear.

"I needed coffee," Dillon explained. The gaze Callie was giving her told her Dillon would have received exactly what she needed if she had stayed in bed. Tomorrow morning she wouldn't make that mistake.

"Callie, dear, can I get you a cup?"

With one last sultry look that said *your loss*, Callie turned her attention to Phyllis. "I'd love one, thank you."

"You two have any plans for today?" Phyllis set the steaming cup in front of Callie.

Dillon couldn't resist a little teasing herself. "Well, what I'd really like to do is—" She stopped when Callie kicked her under the table and gave Callie a two-can-play-at-this-game look. What she really wanted to do was go back upstairs and make love all day, and Callie's panicked expression said she was afraid Dillon would actually say just that.

"Whatever you and Bill want, Phyllis."

Callie gave her a good-answer nod.

The four of them strolled through some of the shops for most of the morning, and in the late afternoon they went deep-sea fishing. Dillon caught several fish, one of which was a barracuda at least forty inches long. Callie landed an amberjack and after forty minutes of struggle finally pulled it in on deck. They had dinner at Anthony's Caribbean Grill, and Dillon dropped a few hundred dollars in the slot machines in the casino at the Atlantis Hotel. They strolled back to the Franklins' condo stuffed, tanned, and tired.

After Callie declined an after-dinner drink, opting for a hot shower instead, Dillon watched her retreat up the stairs and kicked herself for not immediately following. Now she would have to wait until it was acceptable for her to go upstairs, all the while picturing

Callie naked with rivulets of water cascading down her smooth body. She had a double.

Dillon finished her drink as quickly as she could, only half paying attention to what Bill was talking about. He was ready to turn in as well, and she forced herself to match his stride as they climbed the stairs. She wanted Callie so badly she wasn't sure she would be able to control herself, imagining Callie lying on the bed under the thin sheet.

Her anticipation increased more every second as she walked down the hall, intending to make love to Callie again. They hadn't said as much, but the way Callie had looked at her all day told her that Callie knew tonight would be a repeat of last. When Dillon finally got into the room she was on fire, and as she closed the door the sound of the lock catching made her mouth dry. There was something inherently sensuous and slightly naughty about locking a door or hanging out the Do Not Disturb sign.

Callie was propped against the headboard, the sheet pulled up just above her breasts. The rapid rise and fall of the fabric clearly indicated she was also ready. The light on the nightstand was on, casting a soft glow over the bed. Dillon slowly crossed the room, each step deliberate in her seduction. Locking eyes with Callie as she moved closer, she slowly removed each piece of her clothing. By the time she stood within arm's reach of Callie, she was naked.

The hunger in Callie's eyes undid her, and when Callie reached for her, Dillon's knees buckled. Callie pulled her onto the bed and rolled on top of her. She smelled like shampoo and soap, and Dillon was suddenly conscious that she smelled like the Franklins' fishing boat. "I need to take a shower."

"Later. What you need is to let me make love to you."

Callie's mouth descended, and when their lips touched, Dillon wrapped her arms around her neck. Callie was a fabulous kisser and Dillon could spend hours simply exploring her lips. Callie nibbled on her bottom lip, then lightly ran her tongue over the edge of it with a deliberate slowness that drove Dillon crazy. She wanted all of Callie's mouth or none, not this teasing, the dangling of ecstasy just out of her reach.

Dillon tried to twist Callie onto her back but Callie was surprisingly strong. "No, you don't. All day I thought of you lying flat on your back in this bed. I plan to kiss every inch of your body from your head to the tip of your toes. Then I'll lick and suck my way back up again. And I might even take a detour right about here for a few days." She slid her fingers into Dillon's center.

Dillon lifted her hips to meet the inquiring fingers but Callie pulled away. Dillon groaned in frustration. One more stroke and she would have come. Callie must have sensed her readiness and pulled out just in time.

Callie did exactly what she said she was going to do, and by the time she finished, every nerve ending in Dillon's body was screaming for release. She had never been so aroused, and if Callie's lovemaking weren't such pleasure, she would be in agony. As it was, she wanted to come so badly all she had to do was close her eyes and envision Callie's head between her legs and she would burst. But as much as she wanted to come, she would not deny Callie what she wanted.

Finally, after what seemed like hours of foreplay, Callie's mouth settled where Dillon needed it the most. She used her fingers to separate the folds of flesh and lightly blew on the hard bud. Dillon moaned and felt Callie smile against her inner thigh. Callie's tongue darted out and flicked her clit once, then twice, followed by long strokes that moved over her. Dillon gripped the sheets, arching her back. Callie looked up at her and simultaneously slid her tongue into her, never breaking eye contact. The sight of Callie watching her while her tongue pulsated in and out of her core was too much. Dillon exploded.

Her hips lifted off the bed, accompanied by Callie's determination to lick and suck the life out of her. She rocked, Callie's tongue matching her thrust for thrust. Dillon lost all track of the here and now as she rode the waves of pleasure crashing over her. Repeatedly she followed the path to oblivion and back again, all under the skillful mouth of Callie Sheffield. The roar in her ears almost deafened her as it grew louder with each approaching climax.

Finally spent, she fell back on the bed barely able to breathe. Dillon didn't know if she'd screamed or not. God, she hoped not, with Bill and Phyllis in the next room. Her throat was dry, but that could have happened when she practically hyperventilated. Callie was still between her legs, depositing soft, gentling kisses on her thighs. When Callie ventured too close to the part of her body that was now too sensitive to be touched, Dillon pulled her up. Callie settled her weight on top of her, sliding her thigh between Dillon's legs high enough to press against her.

Callie was breathing almost as fast as Dillon, and her body was covered in a light sheen of sweat. Dillon ran her fingers over the hard back and into her damp hair. She pulled Callie's head from where it rested on her shoulder and kissed her. She tasted herself on Callie's lips and her desire began to rise again. Dillon had to have her, and she had to have her now.

This time when Dillon rolled Callie onto her back she didn't resist, but pulled Dillon's head to her breasts. Dillon feasted on the warm flesh, teasing each nipple to erectness and then teasing it some more. With each nip and suck Callie moaned and moved her hips toward Dillon in the universal symbol for release. Dillon wanted to give to Callie as much as she had received, but she sensed Callie couldn't wait. She lightly bit on one nipple while she slid two fingers deep inside.

Warmth wrapped around her fingers and a surge of wetness spilled into her palm. When she found Callie's pleasure point with her thumb, the flesh around her fingers tightened and Callie's pulse beat rapidly. She wanted Callie, had to taste her, had to have the very last drop of her. Dillon shifted, and when she replaced her thumb with her mouth, Callie whispered her name as she climaxed.

The sound of her name falling from Callie's lips was as soft as the wind blowing through the trees. Dillon felt as if she had come home. She was right where she wanted to be. She was awed by the power this simple physical act of one body touching another could have on her. Sex had always been pleasurable, but she had never felt as powerful yet vulnerable as she did right now. Callie was a desirable, passionate lover. Making love to Callie was more than just a physical release. It was spiritual, and Dillon could see herself doing it over and over every night for a very long time.

❖

Phyllis leaned back against the counter, looking at Dillon as she nursed her coffee. "You know, when you get to be my age you get a free pass to say whatever you want," Phyllis said after a few minutes of silence.

"And what's that, Phyllis?" Between not enough sleep and Callie's naked body upstairs in their warm bed, Dillon wasn't very sharp this morning. Otherwise, she might not have invited Phyllis to continue.

"Are you going to marry that girl?"

Dillon choked on her coffee and it dribbled down her chin. She reached for a napkin before it could drop on the counter. "I beg your pardon?"

"You heard me. I've seen a lot in my time, and I know when people are happy and are meant to be together. I saw it from the very first day with Haley and Tammy, and I see it with you and Callie. I can't miss the way you two look at each other. It's like you want to disappear inside each other. I bet the sex is fabulous."

Dillon choked again. "Jesus, Phyllis, will you give some advance notice before you drop another bomb?" If they had been talking about her professional life, she wouldn't be so rattled. But Dillon wasn't used to talking about her personal life or, rather, having someone tell her about it. Shit, she'd never cared what people thought about it.

Phyllis continued as if she hadn't heard a word Dillon said. "You two were made for each other." Phyllis turned serious. "Dillon, don't throw this opportunity away. Haley and Tammy lost the chance to be happy with the person they loved. Don't let that happen to you and Callie."

Phyllis said the words so fast, Dillon wasn't sure she heard them correctly. Did Phyllis wake up this morning with Alzheimer's? She had never mentioned anything about her and Callie being together. But not only had Phyllis just said what was on her mind, she was waiting for an answer.

"Phyllis, don't you think this is a little sudden?"

"No, as a matter of fact, I don't. Call it old-lady syndrome, but I care for you, Dillon, and I care for that girl. She's been through a lot with her useless parents and the awful situation her brother is in. She needs you, Dillon. She needs your support, your strength, and, most important, your love. Don't let her slip through your fingers."

Between bouts of lovemaking last night, Callie told Dillon that she had confided in Phyllis about her mother and Michael after dinner. She said she hadn't portrayed herself as a victim in either case but simply said her situation was a fact of life. Both Bill and Phyllis had given her unconditional support and told her if she ever needed anything, to please let them know. Dillon knew they were talking about money for Michael's defense.

"Let what slip through your fingers?" Bill asked, walking into the room smelling of aftershave.

Phyllis kissed her husband on the cheek. "Callie. I was just telling Dillon she'd better not let that girl get away. She needs to marry her."

Bill laughed and gave his wife a playful hug. "You have to excuse my wife, Dillon. She's a dyed-in-the-wool romantic, and that's why I love her. She thinks everyone is destined for happily ever after." He stopped and looked at her critically. "But in this case I think she's right. I'd love to see you two together." He paused a moment, then looked her right in the eye. "And I have the perfect wedding gift."

Dillon hid her reaction to Bill's last comment. Was he trying to tell her something? Did he just drop his four acres into her lap? She returned his gaze with unwavering eyes and searched for any sign that this wasn't what she thought it was.

She was usually good at reading people, but Bill had thrown her a curveball and her patience snapped. She was tired of being strung along. They had been dancing around the bush with this deal and she had had enough. She needed to get on with this project or bail out altogether, and she couldn't do that. It meant too much to her.

"I couldn't agree with you more, Bill."

Chapter Thirteen

I now pronounce you married in the eyes of the Lord, your friends, and family. You may kiss the bride."

Dillon turned from the elderly gentleman wearing a white collar to the woman in the pale blue dress who stood beside her. Callie Sheffield was arguably the most beautiful woman Dillon had ever seen. Crystal-clear blue eyes looked at her expectantly. A shy smile she had come to know over these past few months held her attention, while a warm hand cupped her face.

"You're supposed to kiss me now."

The voice was soft and melodious, teasing in its inflection. Callie—insightful, intuitive, and always right—was one of the few people Dillon Matthews allowed to actually tell her what to do. She knew how to listen to those around her, especially when they knew more about something than she did.

She bent her head and kissed the red lips as instructed, and a wave of heat practically welded her feet to the floor. The taste of Callie's lips made her forget where she was and how long she stood there.

Finally, she released them and faced the crowd of people who sat in the church's hard-backed pews. Some were friends, others were business associates, and dozens were people she had never seen before.

She took a deep, shaky breath. By all accounts this should have been the happiest day of her life, but as she gazed at the sixty faces that stared back at her, all she could think was, "How in the hell did I get here?"

Callie's grip was tight on her arm. Callie, her *wife*. The past few months flashed through Dillon's mind as she walked down the aisle toward the back of the small church in the quaint town of St. Charles. Callie wanted to be away from the hustle and bustle of Chicago, and Dillon had readily agreed. Even though she wasn't in love with Callie and the ceremony was just another means to the end, she didn't want a bunch of people she knew watching her practically bastardize the sanctity of marriage. She was glad that her side of the chapel held more of the overflow from Callie's side than her own guests.

The three months that had passed since her conversation with Phyllis and Bill at their beach house in the Bahamas had been filled with nothing but Callie and had led up to today. Dillon had spent almost all her free time courting Callie—going for long walks and eating pizza in the middle of the night after making love instead of making dinner. They sat together on the couch, Callie with the latest lesbian bestseller, Dillon with her briefcase. On more than one occasion they went to bed and simply held each other until they fell asleep.

One night about three weeks after they returned from the beach, Callie lay spent on top of Dillon, their bodies flushed and sweaty. "Will you marry me?"

"What?" Callie lifted her head off Dillon's shoulder.

"Will you marry me?" The second time she said it came out a lot more easily than the first. She had given the decision a lot of thought, definitely to the point of distraction. It was simple, really. Bill and Phyllis had weaved their way into their lives, and they had expressed their wish to see her and Callie together. So Dillon kept seeing her. It wasn't a hardship, far from it. Callie was undemanding, fun, a good conversationalist, and fabulous in bed.

It didn't take long for Dillon to figure out that the Franklins were living their granddaughter's life through her and Callie. In a way Dillon pitied the older couple. They had other children and grandchildren, but the death of Haley had affected them deeply and they chose to get on with their life vicariously. Dillon wanted what

Bill had. They wanted what she had. It was a perfect match and, after all, wasn't this really just business?

Dillon had been seeing Callie exclusively, and theirs was by far the longest relationship she'd had in a long time. Usually she got so busy she didn't have time to spend time with whomever she was dating and simply lost interest. But she made time to see Callie. They had lunch together when they could both get away, and when Dillon was in town they had dinner out or Callie cooked. Their evenings were filled with good food, laughter, and lovemaking. Even Greg noticed the change in her. He ventured to ask about Callie one afternoon when Dillon left before he did, which was rare. She had to keep the charade going. Too much was riding on it not to.

Dillon's heart beat faster when Callie hesitated, a reaction she certainly hadn't expected. She had never proposed before and didn't have a perspective, but she thought she knew how Callie felt about her.

Neither of them had said the three magic words, but Dillon knew Callie wanted to. She had seen her pull the words back into her mouth on more than one occasion, and even though she wasn't in love with Callie, she would say them if she needed to. She needed to finish this project. This deal was killing her and she needed to act now. It was business, and she always took care of business.

"Dillon, I can't marry you."

Dillon didn't expect Callie to say no. She had swept her off her feet and showed her what life could be like with her. Callie needed her and she was willing to help her with her problems. "Why not?"

"Because I just met you."

Dillon thought fast. She had to counter her argument. Something told her that if she could get Callie to commit, Bill would sign the papers. The clock was ticking and the longer the delay, the more it cost her. If she didn't get this issue resolved in the next two months, she would have to pull the plug on Gateway. And that was not acceptable.

"So? I want you in my life, Callie. I don't want to be with anyone else. I want you, only you." That was about the best she could do right now.

"Callie?" When she still didn't answer, Dillon pulled the final ace from her sleeve. "I can help you with Michael's defense. We can hire the best appellate attorney money can buy. Let me help you with this, Callie. Marry me."

Callie almost forgot to breathe. Her ears were still ringing from her climax, and she shook her head a few times to clear them. Had she heard Dillon correctly? She had even asked her to repeat what she'd said, and she still wasn't sure she heard right. Admittedly, she had dreamt this, even gone so far as to fantasize what it would be like to be committed to Dillon, but she never thought it would actually happen. From what she could put together, Dillon was married to her job. But lately even that didn't make sense. Hell, nothing made sense anymore.

She continued to stare at Dillon and felt as if she had just asked her to jump out of a perfectly good airplane with no parachute. Well, hadn't she? The analogy certainly fit. Wasn't that what love was all about? Jumping out of a stable life into the unknown with absolutely no guarantees? She lifted herself off Dillon's warm body and sat up. She pulled the sheet around her and felt ridiculous at her modesty at the same time. But she felt vulnerable, more vulnerable than she ever had, and she needed the psychological safety the thin material provided. Dillon sat up against her headboard.

Dillon was everything Callie wanted in a woman, but it was too soon. They had known each other less than six weeks. How could she make this kind of move? Dillon had driven her around the city one weekend to show her the buildings she owned there and pictures of others in different locations. But Dillon's family and friends were still practically strangers to her.

However, she needed to consider Michael. Dillon had accompanied her to Lompak last week. The prison allowed two visitors per prisoner per week, but she waited outside while Callie visited with her brother. Dillon was right, she could help Michael. He needed a good attorney and Dillon could give that to him. *She* could give that to him. "Yes."

And the wedding plans began. Now here they were two months later, shaking hands with friends, family, strangers, and the Franklins, who had integrated themselves into their lives and wedding plans seamlessly.

Callie thrived on the attention Phyllis gave her, and her confidence grew. She accepted Phyllis and Bill as the parents she never had, and Dillon and Bill seemed to genuinely like each other. Phyllis acted as if she were actually the mother of the bride. She and Callie pored over bridal books and flower arrangements, toured countless churches and reception halls. Amazingly, Callie even found time and inspiration to paint again. She had recently completed a landscape that captured the first morning in the Bahamas on the Franklins' patio. It would be her wedding present to Dillon.

Callie asked Dillon to choose the dress she wanted Callie to wear, and one night, with Callie holding Dillon's orgasm literally in the palm of her hand, Dillon finally agreed to wear a tuxedo.

Dillon shook the last hand in the reception line. "Now what?"

Callie laughed and put her arm through her wife's. Her wife. What a wonderful sound. She was Mrs. Dillon Matthews. She could barely believe it. One minute she was struggling to pay the rent, the next married to one of the wealthiest women in the country. How she got there was a story she couldn't wait to tell her grandchildren, but she knew what she needed to do to stay. Callie loved Dillon, plain and simple, and she would do anything to keep them as happy as they were right now.

"We go inside and dance, silly. Didn't you listen to anything I said about today?"

Why was Dillon so distracted? Was she really that nervous? She had seemed relatively calm this past week while she and Phyllis dealt with one minor wedding crisis after another. They were the ones who should be anxious. Practically all Dillon needed to do was show up.

Dillon put her hand over Callie's and smiled down at her. "Of course I did. I just don't remember what you said."

They walked arm in arm into the reception hall. Theoretically, this was supposed to be the happiest day of her life. In actuality Dillon was ecstatic. The contract Bill had signed to sell his property was sitting on her desk at home. The long wait was almost over.

Until the property closed escrow and was recorded with the county, she needed to convincingly play along. She planned to wait an acceptable length of time before she told Callie she had fallen out of love with her. Callie would take it badly, but in the end it would be the right thing to do. Callie would not want to stay with a woman who didn't love her.

"What am I going to do with you, Ms. Matthews?" Callie faked annoyance.

"Dance with me," Dillon replied as they stepped onto the hardwood floor. The first dance was saved for the bride and groom, and even though this was not a typical wedding, Callie and Dillon danced alone. They fit like two pieces of clay molded together to form a striking couple. Callie's dress reflected the blue in her eyes while Dillon had chosen a green tie to accentuate the darkness in hers. They swept around the dance floor oblivious to anyone other than each other.

"Everyone's watching us. You're supposed to look adoringly into my eyes and kiss me now," Callie teased.

"What? I'm sorry, what did you say?" Dillon chastised herself. She held a beautiful blonde in her arms and her thoughts kept returning to the signed document on the desk in her study. She needed to get her head in the here and now, not twenty-three months from now when Gateway opened with its first tenant.

"I said you're supposed to kiss me. I'm your bride and this is our first dance as a married couple. It's tradition."

Dillon smiled at Callie's seriousness. "In case you haven't looked too closely, we are anything but traditional."

Callie didn't care. This was her wedding too, and she wanted it to be as special and memorable as she had always planned it to be. Before she realized she was a lesbian she dreamed about marrying the perfect man and living happily ever after. Her wedding would be similar to this, but she would have six bridesmaids, a ring bearer, and a flower girl, and her father would walk her down the aisle in her white gown with receding train.

But what she got was quite different. Audrey was her one and only bridesmaid, no children attended her, and she walked down the aisle by herself, sad that Michael was not with her but elated to be marrying Dillon nonetheless. However, the end result was the same. She was married to the woman she loved.

"No, but we are dancing and I do want to kiss you, so why not kill two birds with one stone?"

Dillon lowered her head and, before she kissed her, said, "My wife, ever so practical." The kiss was long and reserved. They were in public, after all, and not in the privacy of her home. A few catcalls circled them, but they were all good-natured and Dillon willingly played along.

Dance after dance they glided across the wooden floor. Several times guests cut in, asking Dillon if they could dance with her bride. It wasn't long before every time someone mentioned the word "bride," her stomach knotted. She was *married*, for God's sake. Never in her life had she expected to be in this position.

A tap on her shoulder drew her attention. Expecting it to be another in the line to dance with Callie, she was surprised to see her sister Laura.

She addressed her question to Callie. "May I dance with your bride?"

Laura often joined them for dinner, and Callie had instantly liked her. Naturally Dillon was left out of the wedding conversations, preferring to work instead. It was one thing to go along with the wedding and another to actively participate.

"Of course you may. But don't keep her too long. I have plans for your sister later." Callie winked at Laura, pecked Dillon on the cheek, walked across the floor, and sat down next to Phyllis.

"Your bride is charming, Dillon. And don't forget about gorgeous. She's hot in that dress."

Dillon stared at Laura and felt as if she had never seen her before.

"Oh, come on, Dillon, don't look at me like that. I may be younger than you but I do know what sex is. I've even had it, several times. As a matter of fact, just this morning—"

"Okay, Laura, I get the picture. And yes, I agree. Callie is beautiful." Dillon led her around a slower-moving couple on the dance floor. "However, I'm not going to discuss my sex life with you. I never did when we were younger and I don't plan to start now."

As teenagers they talked long into the night, when they weren't fighting over clothes and the telephone. One night when Laura was eleven, out of nowhere she asked Dillon if she was "gay." Dillon was too stunned to answer, but Laura told her that it didn't matter if she was, that she would always love her.

At the time Laura asked the question, Dillon was not yet ready to put a name on what she was just beginning to realize herself. Somehow her little sister had been able to see through Dillon's words and actions and ask a simple question that turned her life around.

Laura swatted her sister on the shoulder playfully. "You're no fun. And speaking of no fun, Dad's watching us."

Dillon didn't bother to look around to find their father. She had barely said anything to him this evening, and he had returned the favor. "Probably comparing my dancing to yours."

"Dillon, that's not fair."

"Come on, Laura. When are you going to open your eyes and see that he's done nothing but compare me to you our entire lives? And I've always come up short. But not this time. After today I have everything I need to make him see that I—"

She stopped herself. Laura knew their father was disappointed that she had not gone into law, and Laura had also been the only one to encourage her to pursue her dream of studying in France. Dillon had long suspected that Laura knew she was subconsciously trying to win their father's approval. "Let's don't discuss Dad right now. I have the second most beautiful woman in the room in my arms, and I want to enjoy myself."

Laura frowned. "What are you talking about?"

Dillon scolded herself for saying too much. "Nothing, it's not important. Where's Tim, by the way?" she asked, hoping the mention of Laura's husband would distract her. It didn't.

"Don't try to change the subject on me, Dillon. Something's going on. You haven't done something stupid, have you?"

Dillon refused to bite. No, it wasn't stupid at all. Actually it was quite brilliant. "Come on, Laura, don't rag me on my wedding day."

She lost a step and almost tripped over Laura's feet. Her *wedding day*. Christ, she had actually gotten married. The finality of her actions flooded her like a tidal wave. She glanced over at Callie, who was laughing at something Bill and Phyllis had said. She was glowing as every bride should on the happiest day of her life.

Oh, my God, what have I done?

❖

Dillon deposited Laura with Tim and headed to her table, signaling the waiter along the way. She needed a drink. Preferably a big one. Something that would make her wake up and realize this was all just a bad dream. Instead, she got a cold dose of reality.

"Callie is a beautiful woman."

The harsh voice over her left shoulder brought back unpleasant memories. Dillon couldn't remember the last time her father paid her a compliment. No matter what she tried, she could never measure up to his expectations. Seventeen years ago, when she told him she was a lesbian, a distasteful look crossed his face, but at least he had the good manners not to outwardly say anything. Instead, he said nothing at all. Not once since had he uttered anything remotely personal to her.

James Matthews elegantly sat down in the chair beside her. His glass was half full, and she suspected it was the only drink he'd had that night. Her father never lost control. His face was tanner than the last time she saw him. He must be spending more time on the golf course, she thought blandly. Since he retired four years ago, he played eighteen holes of golf at least three times a week, sometimes more. He still had the sleek, ramrod straight body he had in his twenties, and other than a trace of gray around the temples, his hair didn't betray the fact that he was sixty-seven. Dillon wasn't certain she wanted him at the wedding, but Callie had insisted. Not wanting to go down the rat hole of her relationship with her father, she acquiesced.

"Yes, she is," Dillon replied, surprised that she actually agreed with him about something. They hadn't had a conversation that didn't end with a huge argument in years. He always had to win. She was definitely her father's daughter.

"A very beautiful woman."

The hair on the back of her neck stood up. Something in his tone, the way he said Callie's name, wasn't right. Her father was a philanderer, which she knew from an incident during her teens. She had gone to his office one day to surprise him with her early admittance to Stanford, and she saw them getting into a cab—her father and the other woman. Dillon hailed a cab also and followed them to the Four Seasons Hotel. They didn't see her. Hell, they were so into each other they wouldn't have seen an elephant in the lobby. The redhead was every bit as tall and glamorous as her mother was not. He thought he was fooling everyone. She often wondered if her mother ever had a clue. Her skin ran cold thinking he had his sights on Callie.

"I'm lucky to have her." Dillon couldn't think of anything else to say.

He nodded, his eyes never leaving Callie. "Yes, any man would be proud to have her on his arm."

That was the crux of everything about her father. He was so into appearance and status that it was almost comical. He had been an attorney all his life, progressing to partner of one of the most prestigious law firms in town. With that position came power, money, and ego. He still had all three.

Even though they had never discussed the topic, Dillon knew her father well enough to understand that he was appalled that a woman as beautiful as Callie would waste herself on another woman. In his opinion all she needed was a good man to show her what she really needed, and most likely he thought he was that man.

"I'm breaking ground on Gateway next month," Dillon stated, to change the subject and get his attention off her wife. It worked.

"Really? How long have you been working that deal? One? Two years now?" Dillon could hear him really say, *It's about time. Anyone else would have Phase I completed by now.*

"Actually, it's been ten months. Bill Franklin's was the last piece of property I needed."

"What was his holdup? He have you by the balls knowing you needed his land?"

Her father was always this crude when he talked to her. He never spoke like this with Laura. "No, not at all. As a matter of fact, we finally settled on a price that I thought was way below the value of the property." She had been shocked this morning when Bill crossed out her offering price and lowered it by several million dollars.

"Must be something wrong with it that you don't know about." Her father was implying that she hadn't done her homework, which was anything but the case.

"There's nothing wrong with the property. Bill just wasn't ready to sell, and no amount of persuasion or money was going to get him to change his mind." Dillon defended Bill with the truth.

"Well, anyone else would have been halfway finished by now." James stood and set his drink on the table. "I think I'll dance with the bride."

He casually strolled over to where Callie was dancing with her boss, Ross, and hesitated only slightly when he asked her to dance. But Callie looked stiff, not flowing and relaxed like she was with all the other guests she danced with.

Dillon signaled the waiter for another drink. Her father was a snake. She knew it, yet she continued to try to get him to approve of her life and her value as his daughter. Whereas other fathers loved their daughters unconditionally, hers was disappointed, probably even embarrassed because she was a lesbian. She was successful in every sense of the word, and she didn't need a shrink to know something was seriously wrong with the fact that she was still looking for her father's approval.

Dillon went in search of her mother, whom she found at the bar. The slight slurring of her words convinced Dillon she wasn't ordering her first or even second cocktail. "Mother, I've been looking for you." She hadn't, but it was a good opening.

"Dillon, there you are. Laura and I have been looking all over the place for you. Tim wants to talk to you about something. I don't remember what." She took the mixed drink from the bartender, and

Dillon signaled him that this was the last drink he would be serving her.

Dillon held her arm as they walked toward Laura and Tim. "I've been talking to Dad."

"Where is your father, anyway? I've barely seen him all night." Marjorie Matthews glanced unsteadily around the room. "There he is, dancing with your Callie. Dillon, I'm still ashamed of you for not telling us you were even seeing someone, let alone serious enough to marry the girl. If I didn't know better I'd say you had to marry her."

Dillon knew her mother had no idea about Bill Franklin and his four acres, but she was sensitive to the comment nonetheless. "Mother."

"Don't 'Mother' me. I admit I don't know what you two do or how you do it, but if you were a man, I would swear that Callie was pregnant and you had to marry her."

"Mother, shotgun weddings went out of style forty years ago." *Or did they?*

Chapter Fourteen

Callie tried hard not to dislike her father-in-law, but he was making it very difficult. From the first time she'd met James, something about him gave her the creeps. She tried not to read too much into his comments or the way he looked at her, but tonight she finally had to admit that he was making a play for her. His hand wandered a little too low for propriety, and when he pulled her closer, the beginnings of his erection made her want to vomit.

"Dillon is finally going to begin her next project." Callie had tried talking about anything and everything, but James gave only one-syllable answers, and those not far from her ear. This topic, however, seemed to pique his interest.

"Yes, she told me. It's about time she got that job going. I don't know what's been taking her so long. She should have had it started months ago."

Callie was relieved that his thoughts had been diverted, at least for the time being. "She was still negotiating with Bill."

"Well, I don't know what she was offering him, but it must have been insulting for it to have taken this long to complete. You can't undercut a deal without it coming back to bite you in the ass."

"I'm certain Dillon did what she needed to. All that matters is that Bill signed the papers this morning and she couldn't be happier." Callie prayed the song would be over soon.

"What about you? Are you happy?"

She pulled away and looked at James, surprised by his question.

"Why wouldn't I be?" She hated answering a question with a question, but she refused to give him anything.

"You're a very beautiful woman, Callie. You could have any man in the room, probably any man you set your sights on." His eyes read her body to emphasize his point.

Now she definitely didn't like him. Dillon had told her of his indifference toward her life and lifestyle, but she didn't expect this treatment. "But I want your daughter." Her response was catty but she didn't care. He had just insulted her and Dillon.

A sour look crossed his face and then was gone. "My point exactly."

Callie had enough of beating around the bush. "James, what are you really saying?"

His expression was calculating. "I'm sure Dillon has told you that I don't approve of her orientation—"

"She never said any such thing. As a matter of fact, she rarely talks about you and Marjorie." *Score one for me.*

Callie had been able to get Dillon to finally talk about her parents only two weeks ago. She had met Laura several times, but never James and Marjorie. Dillon had described her parents as "difficult." At first Callie thought she was simply estranged from them, but after spending a few hours with them yesterday, and this today, she agreed with Dillon.

Without saying so, Marjorie espoused the belief that you could never be too rich or too thin. Her demeanor was as brittle as her bones appeared to be, and Callie wouldn't be surprised to see her face crack if she even ventured to smile. She was so tight and cold that the temperature dropped by several degrees when she walked into the room.

James was arrogant. Obviously he was used to the people around him, Marjorie included, jumping at his every command. He had been barely civil at dinner last night, and today he was even worse, practically ignoring Dillon. Callie had watched him with his other daughter, Laura, whom he obviously doted on. His face lit up whenever she spoke or he looked at her. Even at twenty-eight she was clearly still Daddy's little girl.

Callie was shocked when it became apparent that Dillon's father barely tolerated her. Had it always been this way? If not, what could have caused the rift between them? James probably was the type of man who believed that having a lesbian daughter indicated something negative about his manhood.

When Dillon's parents walked into the restaurant last night, Dillon had visibly changed. The self-assured, successful woman disappeared, and a nervous, unfamiliar person who deferred to James—his opinions and his domination of the conversation—emerged. The entire evening this new version of Dillon had tried to get her father's attention, his *real* attention, not just the superficial I-know-you're-there variety. Her attempt wasn't overt, and anyone else observing them probably wouldn't have noticed. But Callie was attuned to the woman she planned to marry the next day, and it was completely obvious that Dillon was desperately seeking her father's love and acceptance.

Callie made love to Dillon that night with a tenderness that she had never expressed. With her body and her soul she tried to use passion and desire to erase the pain she saw in Dillon's eyes. She worshipped her strong body, Dillon crying out in ecstasy several times throughout the night. Callie's heart broke for Dillon but she never spoke of her sorrow.

"Then why are we here?" James rudely asked.

"Because I encouraged her to invite you." Sometime during the discussion the song had changed and she missed her opportunity to escape from his grasping hands.

"So I should thank you?"

"No. Dillon makes her own decisions. If there's anyone you should thank, it's her."

"Why do you want to be with a woman? What does Dillon have that any good man couldn't give you?"

Callie knew he meant what *he* could give her. Men like James had come on to her before. This type just didn't get it. They thought with their dicks and believed love was sex. This was a crucial moment for her and her future relationship with her in-laws. If she said what was on the tip of her tongue, her remark would cause a strain in their marriage for quite some time. If she kept her mouth shut and acted as though she didn't know what he was talking about, she would be a hypocrite.

"Is Dillon adopted?" He looked as if her question caught him off guard. She repeated it.

"Of course not. Why do you even ask?" James asked, as if he would rather cut off his arm than raise another man's child.

Callie couldn't stop herself. He was on the verge of ruining the happiest day of her life, and she was pissed. "Because she is nothing like Marjorie and absolutely nothing like you, thank God. She is more man than you will ever be and more woman than you will ever have." Callie dropped her arms and left him standing on the dance floor, and she didn't care who saw what she had done.

Dillon had her back to the dance floor, so she missed the show, but Laura didn't. "Callie doesn't look happy."

Dillon turned in her chair just as Callie approached. The anger in her face was obvious, and when Dillon saw her father standing alone in the middle of the floor, she knew why. "Would you excuse us for a minute, Laura?"

She grasped Callie's hand and escorted her to the patio. "What's wrong? What did he say?" Dillon wasn't sure she wanted to know the answer to her questions, but she needed to defend her wife.

Callie fought to remain in control. She was so angry and hurt that she didn't know if she should cry or throw something, preferably at her father-in-law. She chose neither. "I owe you an apology."

"For what?"

"For badgering you to invite your parents. I should have let it go the first time you told me you didn't want them here."

Dillon looked furious, as if she would like to wring her father's neck. "What did he say to you, Callie?"

"It's not important." Callie shook off her mood. This was her wedding day, and it was all about her and Dillon.

Dillon searched Callie's face for any sign that she needed to push a little harder to find out what she and her father had talked about.

"Let it go. Dillon, please, for me."

Obviously James had said something to upset Callie, and Dillon was irritated that Callie wouldn't tell her. She knew better than most that her father could be cruel and downright ugly. The remarks he could have made to upset Callie were endless. But if Callie wanted to forget about the incident and move on, she would try to as well. She looked at Callie's hand on her arm and put on her best smile. She filed the conversation she planned to have with her father in the back of her mind and wondered why she was willing to confront her father about his treatment of Callie when she wouldn't do the same for herself.

"All right, if you insist."

"I do. All that matters is that I love you, I'm your wife, and you better take me home before we consummate this marriage right here on the patio."

Callie's smile was brilliant. Dillon's heart melted just a little, and the familiar tingling in the pit of her stomach jumped to life. The more times they were together, the more overwhelming her desire for Callie became. They had made love countless times in the last few weeks, each time more powerful than the last. Every time with Callie was like the first time, and Dillon craved her touch, her smell, her taste.

Callie knew just how to please her. She knew when to go slow and when Dillon needed it hard and fast. Her tenderness was breathtaking, and last night Dillon had sensed a side of her she hadn't seen so far. Her touch was soothing, like a cool cloth on a hot day. Slowly she had stoked the fire between them until finally, after hours, she allowed Dillon to orgasm. She played her body like a symphony, each touch and kiss taking her higher and higher until she thought she couldn't go any further, and with one final touch Callie took her over the top. She made Dillon's body explode, leaving her mind mush long after her orgasm subsided. And then Dillon had wanted Callie again.

"Yes, ma'am, whatever you say." Dillon laughed. "My God, I'm already henpecked."

It took another hour to politely say good-bye to their guests. Dillon wanted to slip out the back, but Callie insisted they had better manners than that. Dillon joked that it wasn't her lack of manners that made her want to be alone with Callie sooner rather than later.

Right before they left, Laura hugged her tight and whispered into her ear, "I'm so happy for you, Dillon. Callie is perfect for you. She's warm and charming and witty and finally somebody who can handle you. Don't do anything to screw this up."

Laura turned her loose. She and Tim were the last ones to leave, her parents and the Franklins having departed twenty minutes earlier. "What do you mean, can handle me? I'm a pushover."

What she was really doing by marrying Callie under these conditions was unmentionable. Sometime during the evening festivities she realized exactly what she had done. She had married someone, made what was supposed to be a lifetime commitment in the name of love into a business deal.

She had pushed the thought out of her mind, preferring to concentrate on the expression on her father's face when he saw Gateway for the first time. The mock-up was complete and dominated a third of her corner office. *That* would be what it was all for.

A sly smile crossed Laura's face. "Uh-huh. I know exactly what she does to push your buttons. Well, not exactly, but I have a general idea."

Dillon laughed, loving her sister more than she ever imagined possible. Laura was her rock, her sense of being when she herself occasionally lost her own sense of self. Her sister loved her in spite of her flaws and transgressions. Sometimes Laura seemed to understand her more fully than she did herself.

❖

Callie sighed, sinking into the soft leather of the limousine seats. She was exhausted, and what little sleep she'd gotten last night was not nearly enough. She leaned her head back onto the seat. The day had been perfect. She felt beautiful, and when she saw Dillon waiting for her at the altar, she wished she had taken Bill up on his offer to walk her down the short aisle. Michael was the man she wanted by her side, and because that was impossible she had chosen to walk alone. She had missed him terribly but recalled the smile that filled his face when she told him of her pending nuptials. Even with Michael in her heart, her legs were weak and she had to concentrate to get down the aisle without falling.

She still could not believe how fast her life had changed. Dillon had practically swept her off her feet, to use a cliché that seemed amazingly accurate, and now here she was, Mrs. Dillon Matthews. She would always remember how Dillon had taken care of everything. She wasn't involved in the details of planning the wedding, but her support was evident everywhere. She had made time in her schedule to meet with the caterer, the musicians, even the lady who set up the tables in the reception hall. One evening soon after Dillon proposed, she'd slipped a credit card into Callie's hand. Callie's name embossed on the platinum American Express card was more than access to Dillon's money. It was access to their life together.

"What are you thinking?" Dillon's voice drifted around her. It was warm and comforted her like a soft blanket.

"Just how happy I am. And worn out," Callie added, smiling.

Dillon slid over and kissed her favorite spot on Callie's neck, just below her ear, and Callie felt her own pulse beneath Dillon's lips begin to beat erratically. She smiled as Dillon lengthened the kiss, then murmured, "Hopefully not too tired. It is our special night, you know."

Dillon had insisted on taking care of all the arrangements for the following week, and hadn't even disclosed where they would spend their wedding night. She told Callie to pack sparingly, teasing her that she wouldn't need many clothes—probably none at all.

Callie's body came alive under Dillon's mouth. She didn't move, but simply enjoyed the sensation of warmth and desire that slowly spread through her. "You know, I read in one of the bridal magazines that most couples don't consummate their marriage right after the wedding because they're exhausted, had too much liquor, or both."

Dillon's hand went under the hemline of Callie's dress and inched up her warm thigh. Callie's pulse skyrocketed and she opened her legs, granting Dillon greater access. Callie desired her touch more than anything else in the world.

"That's because they didn't just marry you."

Callie shuddered when Dillon's mouth traced a path over her bare shoulders while her fingers followed the smooth seam outlining the crotch of her panties. Her clit was hard, pushing on the damp material as if it were reaching for Dillon's touch. She didn't have to wait long before Dillon's skillful fingers found it and gently flicked the tight flesh. Callie grabbed Dillon's head in both hands and dragged her mouth to hers. She kissed her long and deeply, her body moving closer to Dillon's exploring fingers. "Touch me, please," she begged. Callie didn't care if the driver could see through the dark privacy window. She was on fire and Dillon was the only one who could ease her torment.

With agonizing slowness Dillon's fingers slid her panties to the side. Callie lifted her ass off the seat, giving Dillon permission to remove them. Dillon made short work of the brief garment, and Callie moaned when her fingers found their mark. Dillon's kisses were deep and passionate, and Callie willingly gave as good as she received. She briefly imagined what they would look like to a casual observer, her dress hiked around her waist, Dillon's tongue in her mouth. The image was erotic and she arched into Dillon's fingers as they entered her. Faster and faster Dillon's hand moved, and soon both women were panting and bucking like this was their first time. Dillon took her higher and higher, alternately stroking and fucking her until Callie finally exploded.

Lights, stars, and a roar like a wind tunnel filled Callie's brain, her senses reacting to Dillon's touch. She alternately floated and returned to earth with each wave of climax. Her thighs quivered and her hands shook as she gripped Dillon's hair. Her breathing was ragged and shallow, and at one point she thought she might hyperventilate. Dillon's fingers were still inside her, and when they started to move again, she shuddered.

"Dillon?" Her name croaked out of Callie's very dry mouth.

"Hmm?"

Callie's head was on the verge of spinning again, and she

had to remind herself what question she intended to ask and, most important, why she wanted to ask it now. "Don't you think we should have waited till we get to wherever we're going?"

"I couldn't wait," she rasped.

Callie couldn't either. Dillon's hands and fingers knew when to be gentle, shift tempo, and go deeper. Dillon took her two, three, four more times, and when Callie thought she couldn't come one more time, she did. Completely spent, she weakly grasped Dillon's hand and removed it from between her legs. And as she did, her fingers brushed across the diamond band on Dillon's left ring finger. It was an exact match to the one Dillon had slipped on her finger a few hours earlier and symbolized Dillon's commitment to her. Dillon pulled her onto her lap and, content, Callie snuggled into her embrace and instantly fell asleep.

Dillon desired Callie like she had never desired another woman. She didn't feel possessive—far from it. She didn't want to own Callie any more than she wanted to own any woman. She craved her, and Callie had proved on over a hundred occasions that she was a more than willing participant.

She gazed at her sleeping bride and thought about how her life had changed so much that she hardly recognized it. She had gone out that night four months ago simply looking to have a good time with a beautiful, willing woman, maybe two, if she was really lucky. And she had ended up with something altogether different.

She had wanted Callie almost immediately. Her reaction was typical, purely physical lust for a beautiful woman, and Callie had certainly filled every criteria. Dillon's body had spoken to her in a familiar language until she read something different on Callie's face. At that moment her mind and body declared war on each other. After that first glimpse of Callie, each time Dillon saw or thought of her, her body ached to explore the soft curves and womanly beauty that Callie so eagerly offered now. She wanted to worship her body, cherish every sight and sound of their lovemaking because it was unlike anything she could have ever imagined.

She wondered for a moment if this was what Laura and Tim's sex life was like. Did they feel the same driving desire to touch one another whenever they were in the same room? She had watched her sister dance with her husband several times tonight, and even when their bodies weren't touching, something was always passing between them. Sex was one of the most powerful cravings a body could have. Without it, she would wither and die.

But sex could also be used as a weapon, and her father wielded it like a knight. This evening was no different, and when he hit on Callie, Dillon wanted to kill him. Her father didn't worship women, the feel of their body, the softness of their skin, the shy little sounds they made in the dark of night. He used women for his own pleasure, ignoring their feelings to get what he desired. She doubted he remembered the name of half of the women he had bedded.

Dillon froze. The pattern was all too familiar. Was she describing him or herself? She couldn't ignore the similarities. No matter how much she despised him and his behavior, she wanted his approval and had become just like him. She looked at Callie. She hadn't married Callie because she loved her and wanted to spend the rest of her life with her. Sure, the sex was fabulous, but she had married her to get what she wanted. As much as she hated the realization, she was just like her father. Her stomach turned. It was the last thing she had expected and the very last thing she wanted.

CHAPTER FIFTEEN

Ten days later, tanned and rested, Dillon opened the door to her office. She had enjoyed her time away more than she anticipated, but was anxious to begin moving on Gateway. Greg jumped up and gave her a big hug. He was rarely this demonstrative in the office, preferring to show his emotions when they were together socially.

Greg's questions rattled off his tongue. "Dillon, you're back. We've all missed you. How's Callie? How was Paris? Did you see the Eiffel Tower and the Leaning Tower of Pisa? Were you decadent, and did you eat and drink your way around the City of Love?"

She smiled and set a brown bag on his desk. "Greg, take a breath, buddy. Callie's fine, Paris is beautiful in the summer, the Eiffel Tower is still there, and the Leaning Tower of Pisa is not in France, it's in Italy. I ate more than I should have, and Paris's legend as the City of Love is still intact."

Dillon had insisted on planning the honeymoon, and the limo had taken her and Callie directly to the airport. A business associate had offered her the use of his private plane and pilot, and Dillon booked it to fly them directly to Paris. If she had to have the honeymoon that everyone expected, why not have it in one of her favorite cities? They made love over the Atlantic and as they circled Paris waiting for clearance to land.

Their days were filled with visiting the typical tourist attractions, and Callie was their tour guide, reading every brochure and placard as they went. She had never been to Paris and was like the proverbial kid in a candy store, wanting to see everything. They stayed at the Novotel Paris Tour Eiffel overlooking the Seine River, and even though they fell into bed exhausted every night, they made love with the lights of the city as their blanket of stars.

"Here, I brought you something." Dillon handed Greg a bag with the familiar Cartier logo on the side. After another round of hugs and at least fifteen minutes ogling his gifts, Greg finally set the black signature-collection desk clock next to his telephone and put the Louis Cartier fountain pen in his pocket.

"Do I dare go inside and look at my in-box?" Dillon asked, nodding toward her private office door.

"Yes. You know I took care of everything while you were gone."

Greg could probably run Matthews Holdings as well as she could, at least the administrative side of it. Hell, he probably already did. "I have no doubt, Greg. What's on my calendar today?"

Dillon had told Greg to keep her schedule light on her first day in the office. Getting back into the swing of the business after ten days wasn't a challenge, but she preferred to spend the first day sorting through her e-mail and the pile of paper that had accumulated in her in-box. The challenge was leaving Callie naked in their bed earlier this morning.

When it was still dark she had woken to Callie's warm lips on her breast and her hand zeroing in on the apex of her legs. Their return flight had been delayed due to airport conditions, and they got in last night quite a bit later than they planned. They collapsed into bed after barely being able to keep their eyes open for a quick good-night kiss. An hour after her very pleasant wake-up call, Dillon had stumbled into the shower, knees still shaking from passion.

Greg began with the most important item. "Bill Franklin's transfer deed is still not ready to be filed with the county commissioner. As soon as it is, you will have clear title and can begin excavation in about six weeks."

Dillon dropped her briefcase on her desk. "Jesus, how long does it take to correct a number, for God's sake. Every day I sit here with my thumb up my butt costs me thousands of dollars. This project has to kick off on time and come in under budget. It's just my luck that some idiot recorded an incorrect parcel number against the original deed. You'd think the commissioner's office could rectify the problem in less than a month."

"So, how is married life?"

How was married life? Besides access to great sex every day, that is? Dillon had thought that the word "commitment" meant duty, confinement, obligation, and a variety of other suffocating adjectives. What surprised her was that so far it had not.

"Great. I suppose it has something to do with the person you marry, but so far so good." She couldn't be overly happy, because in a few months she would have to start dropping subtle hints that all was not well on the home front.

"Do you feel any different? I mean, so many people say that marriage makes them a different person. And how many people do we know who have lived together for years, and once they get married, everything goes to hell?"

Dillon did feel different. "Content" was the best word she could find to describe her state of mind, but she couldn't put her finger on why. She assumed it was because Bill had signed the papers and she could get on with her project. Her plans had been on hold for so long it felt good to get moving again. Callie probably had a little something to do with the pleasant feeling too.

"I suppose I do. More settled, I guess. Looking for the next thing less and enjoying what I have now more. You know, that sort of thing."

"Well, you look great."

She felt great too. Maybe time away was exactly what she needed. Of course, having a beautiful woman on her arm certainly didn't hurt either.

❖

For the first time in years, Dillon invited her father to lunch. She had discussed the possibility with Callie one evening and was not surprised when she said that she would support any decision Dillon made. She had been discussing things with Callie a lot lately. In the few weeks after they had returned from their honeymoon they had fallen into a pattern of taking a walk after dinner, and usually during that time Dillon opened up about her day. Callie listened carefully and asked intelligent questions, and soon Dillon was asking for her advice. Callie was still working at the flower shop, and Michael's appeal was steadily grinding through the judicial system. His attorney was optimistic that he would be granted a new trial within a few months.

Callie was painting more, and often Dillon would wake up to find that after they had made love Callie had returned to the room she had converted into her studio. She had filled canvas after canvas with images of the places they had gone together. The lights of Paris were captured beautifully in one, lovers walking along the Seine in another, and several others simply radiated joy. Dillon had subtly inquired if Callie was interested in a showing and was surprised when she said she had been thinking about it. Dillon knew of several gallery owners and had a note in her calendar that Callie planned to meet with one of them next week.

In the restaurant, her father sat across from her, and Callie was on her right. Dillon felt as if Callie had been beside her for more than just a few weeks. She had become a fixture in her life that Dillon had not expected to need. They chatted on the phone at least once a day, and she hurried home to her every night. Her life had fallen into a comfortable routine, and occasionally Dillon wondered what it would be like once Callie was gone.

After lunch, Callie and James drank coffee in Dillon's office as Dillon showed off the mock-up of Gateway. Callie was amazed at what Dillon had accomplished in her life and even prouder that Dillon's Gateway was finally becoming reality. She had worked tirelessly the past few months to make her dream come true, and Callie couldn't have been more proud of Dillon than she was today.

As she watched Dillon point out the specifics of each structure to her father, she wanted to pinch herself to make sure she wasn't imagining this new life. It had been five months since she met Dillon, and sometimes she managed not to be afraid that she would wake up and find it had all been a dream. Except for early this morning when Dillon wasn't beside her, but between her legs waking her in a way that was so much better than a cup of coffee. She was in love with Dillon and knew Dillon loved her because she had given her everything she could possibly imagine. Callie was the happiest person on earth.

But James's presence threatened to ruin the day. He was his typical caustic self that she had come to expect after having several dinners with him and Marjorie. It hurt her to know that he didn't share her pride in Dillon or her accomplishments. Dillon was a wonderful person, whom any man other than James Matthews would be proud to call his daughter. Dillon had not come out and said so specifically, but Callie knew Gateway was the plan Dillon hoped would win her father's approval. It was huge, expensive, and cutting-edge architecture, but James's mannerisms and lack of interest clearly indicated he was anything but impressed.

Thankfully James didn't stay long. Callie didn't know how much longer she could stand to be in the room with him and his superior attitude and watch her lover's heart break. James didn't bother to close the door behind him, and Callie slid behind Dillon, wrapped her arms around her, and pressed her cheek in her hair. "I'm so happy for you, Dillon."

Dillon barely felt Callie behind her. Her father's reaction, or rather his lack of reaction, to Gateway didn't surprise her, but it did hurt. Jesus, what did he want from her? What did she have to do to get his approval? And why was it so important that she did? "At least somebody is."

"Dillon, your father is an ass. Pure and simple. He wouldn't know a good thing if it bit him on the balls. He's a cynical bastard, and even though he is your father I don't think he's worth the time of your day. I always wanted a father, but if mine were as awful as yours, I wouldn't want him."

Dillon began to relax, but just slightly.

"Tell you what. I've got to run to the ladies' room and then you can walk your beautiful wife to her car. Maybe we can even slip away for a few hours." One hand went north on Dillon's body, the other south to emphasize Callie's suggestion.

"Sure, why not. Let me check my e-mail and I'll be ready when you get back." Callie was making an effort to cheer her up, and Dillon wanted to see her happy.

"Everybody leave?" Greg asked, stepping into her office. "Sorry I wasn't at my desk when you got back from lunch."

"Callie's in the ladies' room and my father just left. He was a ball of laughs, as usual." Dillon looked up when Greg didn't reply. "What is it, Greg? You've got that look on your face that says you want to say something but aren't sure if you should. Come on, out with it." Dillon waved her hand at him.

"I didn't think you would actually go through with it."

Greg knew what Dillon had done to clench Franklin's land. She had confided in him one day when he questioned her about an e-mail he had read from her to Bill, which talked about signing the deed on the day of the wedding. Dillon had printed it and in the margin written *payment for marriage*, and Greg asked what was going on. Dillon told him the entire story. Although he seemed surprised, Dillon knew that he understood her well enough to realize he couldn't stop her.

"Why not? You know how much I needed that property. Bill didn't want to sell to me, and I found the button that needed to be pushed and got it. Couldn't ask for a better wedding present."

"But to marry somebody. Even I think that's going too far in the name of business."

"That's the difference between you and me, Greg. I'd do anything for this project, including marrying Callie. It's just business."

A gasp from the doorway drew Dillon's attention from her keyboard. Callie stood there with her hand over her mouth, and by the look on her face, she had heard more than enough. The cat was out of the bag.

"Callie." Dillon rose and Greg slipped out the side door of Dillon's office.

"I'm a business deal?"

Callie had heard Dillon and Greg talking when she came back

from the ladies' room, and for an instant she thought about waiting in the outer office to give them some privacy, but her legs froze when she heard the conversation. Now she wasn't sure if she should have made the other choice.

"Callie, it's not like that." Dillon scrambled out from behind her desk. She didn't get far before Callie stalked toward her.

"Then what exactly is it? What am I? A merger? An acquisition? A joint venture? What would you call it, Dillon? And by the way, are Bill and Phyllis in on this?" Callie was surprisingly calm. She should be falling apart, but her mind was functioning and her hands were steady.

"No, they don't know anything about it."

Dillon winced, and now Callie was appalled. Dillon had just confirmed that their relationship was anything but love.

"Who did, besides you and Greg?" When Dillon didn't answer, Callie became livid. "Answer me," she said loudly.

"No one."

"So you orchestrated this entire charade? Well, let me tell you something, Dillon. You are absolutely pitiful. I was wrong at our wedding when I told your father you were nothing like him. I was wrong, very wrong. You're exactly like him. But then again, how would I know? You came in like a knight in shining armor saving me from myself, dangling the promise of happily ever after in front of me. Only it wasn't a promise, was it, Dillon?" Callie spoke forcefully in spite of her anger and hurt. "And when I didn't immediately say yes to your proposal, you tossed in the one thing that you knew would get me."

Callie strode to within inches of Dillon. She looked in her eyes for any redeeming value and, seeing none, slapped her. "You bitch."

CHAPTER SIXTEEN

Callie was reeling from her conversation with Dillon. It wasn't a conversation at all, as she had barely given Dillon a chance to speak. But she wouldn't have believed Dillon, whatever she said. The heels of her loafers clicked on the cement as she stormed down the sidewalk with no specific destination in mind. Her mind was spinning and tears blurred her vision, threatening to spill out and slide down her cheeks.

Dillon had used her, plain and simple. She used her to get what she wanted. Well, she got what she wanted, but it certainly wasn't what Callie signed up for. She stopped and put her hand over her mouth, almost oblivious to the people jostling her as they rushed past. Dillon had made love to her, touched her in ways she had never imagined. She felt cheap and dirty. Suddenly she needed to vomit.

Spitting out the last of the bile, Callie leaned back on her heels. Her knees were wet from the grass and her hands shook as she wiped her mouth. She had barely managed to reach the park before the contents of her stomach emptied. Her head was pounding and several people slowed down as they walked by, but nobody offered to help.

What would she say? *No, I'm fine. Just a little miscommunication between me and the woman I married. No big deal, really. Seems as though we had a difference of opinion of what marriage was all about. I thought it meant that you love, honor, and cherish, but she thought it was just a simple business contract. Silly me.*

She staggered to her feet, fighting off another wave of nausea. As she retraced her steps to the parking garage, she stopped when she realized she had run out of Dillon's office without her purse. She had no way to get home. The keypad on the outside of the garage would get her inside once she was there, but home was the last place she wanted to be.

She had rented out her house when she and Dillon got married. She didn't have many possessions, and she'd packed what she wanted to take with her in boxes and stacked them neatly in a corner of Dillon's garage. The phone on her hip vibrated and Callie froze. What if it was Dillon? What if it wasn't? She flipped it open and pushed the talk button.

"Audrey," Callie said into the receiver, leaning against a newspaper stand to regain her balance.

"Hey, babe, how's my happily married best friend?"

"Can you come and get me? I'm at..." Callie looked around to get her bearings. She had no idea how long she had been walking or how far, but she was at least a mile from Dillon's office. "Berkshire and Seventy-fifth Street."

"Callie, what's wrong?"

"Please, Audrey, can you just come pick me up?" Her own voice sounded flat and emotionless, even to her.

"Of course, I'll be there in twenty minutes. Are you all right, Callie? Are you hurt?"

Callie heard the concern in her voice. "I'm fine." Unless you called being bought and used a normal everyday occurrence.

Audrey was true to her word, and Callie was buckled into her front seat twenty minutes later. Mercifully Audrey drove with lightning speed to her apartment without asking any questions. Callie didn't know if she would be able to answer them if she did. Her mind was absolutely blank, and Audrey had to pull over to the side of the road twice for her to throw up again. She was a mess.

Callie didn't remember climbing the stairs to Audrey's apartment, but when she woke several hours later she was lying in the guest bedroom with the covers tucked around her. Her clothes were laid neatly on the chair, and she wore a pair of shorts and one of Audrey's Harvard T-shirts. As she swung her legs over the side of the bed, her head pounded. She gave herself a few minutes for the world to stop spinning before she walked into the bathroom to wash her face and brush her teeth. Feeling halfway human she ventured down the hall.

The television was on and Audrey had her feet propped up on the coffee table. She was flipping through the channels when Callie sat on the couch. "Hey, how are you doing?"

Callie tried to say something but her throat was raw, so she nodded instead. She supposed she was okay, but she was too numb to tell if anything other than her head and throat hurt. When Audrey picked her up she was only able to tell her that she was physically okay.

Audrey went into the kitchen and returned with a mug of hot tea, then sat beside her on the couch. "Wanna tell me about it?" Audrey handed her the mug.

Callie didn't know if she did or not. She was humiliated to have been played like that. The old saying that love is blind was definitely true in her case. She had either missed all the signs or Dillon was good, very good. She was mortified when she thought about the dozens of times they had made love. Was she faking that too?

Audrey must have read the look on her face because she took her hand. "Is it Michael?"

Audrey had been in the courtroom with her every day as well as when the final verdict came in. She knew how close she and Michael were and how devastated Callie was when he was sentenced.

"No," she croaked, and shook her head to reinforce her answer.

"Then what is it, Callie?"

Callie could never resist Audrey's kind voice and calm demeanor. She had always been able to open up to her, even when she didn't want to admit things to herself. This was one of those times. Callie knew she owed Audrey an explanation, and she steeled herself for what she had to say. She drank her tea, each swallow fortifying her courage. When she spoke, she did so calmly and without tears.

"Holy crap, Callie. I don't know what to say except that Dillon is a shit. A first-class, number-one S-H-I-T." When Audrey was really upset, she spelled.

Telling Audrey was the therapy Callie needed to get back in control. "I can think of several other words that would aptly describe her, but that should be enough, at least for now."

"What are you going to do?" Audrey asked, falling back on the couch now that Callie's confession was over.

"Besides trying to keep myself from killing her? I don't know," Callie said seriously. "I can barely think clearly. I have no idea what I want to do next, let alone what I have to do." She looked at her hands, fingers interlocked. The diamonds in her wedding ring winked at her as if to say, "I knew it." Callie slid the ring off her finger. The cool air hit the skin that had already become accustomed to the band, causing her to shiver. "I can't stay there anymore."

"You can stay here as long as you want to."

Callie could always count on Audrey, but her invitation sounded good just the same. "I don't have any clothes." With everything that had happened today, the state of her wardrobe sounded trivial. Again Audrey came to her rescue.

"You can wear mine until you get your stuff. You *are* going to get your things, aren't you?" Audrey asked the question in a tone that made it sound like she thought Callie might go back to Dillon.

That would never happen. Dillon didn't love her. She had married her out of convenience and necessity. Callie refused to be someone's arranged bride, no matter who the woman was. She still had her pride and dignity, even if they were bruised.

"I can't stay married to her. Our relationship is a sham and I won't be any part of it." The impact of her words sank into her brain. Dillon must have wanted Bill's land pretty badly to actually go through with their marriage. Granted, it was more symbolic than legal, but it was a big deal nonetheless. Thank God they didn't need to get a divorce, at least not legally. The last thing she wanted was to have to sit in the same room with someone who had made a fool of her and hash out a property settlement. That would be too humiliating.

Callie had almost forgotten Audrey's original question. "I'll go tomorrow when she's at work, if you can take me. I know she has a couple of meetings across town, so that lowers the possibility of running into her at the house. You can drop me off to get my car when we're done."

She absolutely didn't want to have to face Dillon again. One side of her brain told her someday she would have to, while the other couldn't find a reason why.

❖

"Callie?" Audrey tentatively asked over coffee and donuts. "Is the deal with Bill Franklin completely wrapped up?"

"What?" Callie had been half listening to Audrey drone on about some crisis at work the day before and only caught Bill's name. She hadn't spoken to Dillon since she walked out of her office three weeks ago, but her cell phone had eight messages that she knew were from Dillon. She was screening her calls, and if she didn't immediately recognize the number, she let the machine roll into voice mail. Audrey's phone number was programmed into Dillon's home phone, and it too rang continuously for the first few days. Callie supposed Dillon had pleaded her case to the answering machine, but she deleted the message as soon as she heard her voice.

Flowers were delivered to Audrey's house every day, and Callie promptly forwarded them to the senior center a few blocks away. She half expected Dillon to turn up on Audrey's doorstep at any time, and she wasn't sure what she would do if she did.

She still wasn't sleeping through the night. It took hours to fall asleep, and once she did her dreams were filled with images of Dillon—where they had gone together, what they had done, her smile, her laugh, her touch. She woke in a sweat either from dreaming of their lovemaking or the final scene in her office.

She had never been so hurt. In the past Callie had several relationships that lasted four or five years, but they always fizzled out along with the sex. Deep down she had known she was running that same risk with Dillon, but she didn't care.

In a very short period of time she had fallen in love with Dillon—head over heels. She couldn't have stopped herself even if she wanted to. Dillon was sweet and kind, and treated her like royalty. She pampered her, doted on her, and made Callie feel like she was the only woman on earth.

Recently, Callie had finally admitted that she had been caught up in the moment and let her heart override her mind. In the last few years, she had given so much of herself to everyone that when she met Dillon she believed it was now her turn, that she deserved Dillon's adoration. Dillon had taken advantage of Callie's exhaustion, financial struggles, loneliness, and concern over Michael. God, how could she have been so stupid?

"I was just wondering if the deal with Bill's land could still fall through," Audrey repeated.

The question made no sense to Callie. "So what if it does?"

Nothing would make Callie happier than to see Dillon's actions blow up in her face. She deserved to lose everything she planned for this deal. Dillon had spent hours poring over blueprints, schematics, and sketches for Gateway. Not only was there a mock-up of the project in her office, but an exact duplicate was in the den in her home. She was constantly tinkering with the elevation of a building or the angle of a rooftop. Gateway was her dream, her baby, and she had to have it.

Obviously, she had done whatever she had to get it, including using her. She probably didn't even think twice about the arrangement. She didn't care who got hurt. Callie was a means to an end, and anyone else affected, namely Michael, was collateral damage.

Michael! Oh, my God, what will happen to Michael now? Dillon was funding his entire defense, which had barely begun. The final decision on whether or not he would receive a retrial was expected any day. If the payments to his attorney stopped, so would he.

"Why do you ask?" Audrey had a peculiar look on her face and Callie immediately saw where she was headed. She stood up and began to pace back and forth around the table. "Oh, no. Don't even think about it." She shook her head for added emphasis.

"Callie."

"No, Audrey, absolutely not. Have you lost your mind?"

"No. Come on, Cal, think about it. You can—"

"I will not prostitute myself to Dillon for Michael." Audrey had accompanied her to Lompak the day before and seen the conditions Michael was under. Audrey had driven while Callie cried during the entire return trip.

"Callie." Audrey tried again.

"No, Audrey." For the first time since she had come to stay with Audrey, Callie felt strong and her conviction was firm. She stood a little taller. "What do you think I am? If I were to go back to Dillon for her wallet, I'd be no better than she is. I will not do it."

"Then what will you do? You don't have the money to pay for Michael's lawyer. This guy is his only hope, and if you're going to put your pride before his chance to—"

Callie exploded and flew across the room, then stopped inches from Audrey's face. "Don't you dare talk to me about what I do or don't do for Michael. He's my brother and he is in prison because of me. Every day I get up when I want, eat what I want, go wherever I want, and fuck whomever I want, while he prays every day he doesn't get raped and has to do everything, absolutely everything, to the sound of a whistle. A whistle, for Christ sake! Like an animal obeying commands. So don't tell me what I should do or not do. You have no idea what you're talking about."

She was practically screaming by the time she finished. Her heart was beating against her ribs and she was light-headed. Michael was her hot button and Audrey had just pushed it.

"Callie, that was uncalled for and you know it. I've always been in your corner when it comes to Michael. Sure, I have no idea what it's like to be you, to live with the guilt you have about what happened. But I'm your friend, and as your friend, it's my job to tell you these things whether you want to hear them or not." Audrey's voice was calm and she spoke so quietly Callie had to strain to hear what she said.

The roaring in her ears was beginning to subside, along with her anger. Shame over what she had just said to Audrey replaced it. "I'm sorry. You're right. I never should have said that. You've been

nothing but wonderful to me and Michael for years. I'm just upset."
Callie plopped into the chair and rubbed her face. "God, that sounds
like a flimsy excuse."

Audrey walked over and put her arms around Callie's neck.
"It's okay, you deserve a little slack. You're not getting rid of me
that easy."

"What am I going to do? I have no place to live. Thank God I
have a job." After their wedding, Dillon had told Callie she didn't
have to work, but she insisted that she wanted to keep her job with
Ross. She loved it and Ross, and not working would make her feel
like a kept woman. She chuckled. So much for that principle. Audrey
hugged her tight, then released her.

"I've already told you that you don't have to worry about a
place to live. I kind of like having a roommate."

Callie grinned. "Yeah, until you bring home some hot chick and
find me eating ice cream out of the container. That's a real romance
killer."

"Who says I haven't already brought someone home?"

They laughed for the first time in days.

CHAPTER SEVENTEEN

Dillon slammed the door behind her. Greg had just told her that Callie still had not called, but the florist had. The manager wanted to know if he should continue to deliver to Audrey's house since the deliveries were continuously refused. She stomped across the large office and tossed her briefcase on the chair in front of her desk.

"Fuck," she shouted, not caring who heard her. She had been saying that word a lot lately. She fucked up by talking about her plan in the office where Callie could and did hear, fucked as in if she didn't do something to get Callie back the entire project might go down the drain, and last but not least, was fucking stupid to ever believe this would really work.

The last three weeks had been the longest of her life. She had followed Callie out the door, but the elevator door had closed in her face with Callie on the other side. She repeatedly poked the elevator button as if by some miracle a car would arrive quicker based on the number of times she hit the button. Dillon briefly considered the stairs but she was fifty floors up. By the time she got to the lobby and ran out to the street, Callie was nowhere in sight.

The look on Callie's face haunted her dreams. In an instant her wife's expression had turned from happiness to confusion, comprehension, hurt, and finally anger. Dillon had never seen such a spectrum as Callie's was the day she learned why she had married her.

Dillon had searched frantically for Callie over the next few days. She was not at work, and Dillon wasn't surprised that Callie wouldn't answer her cell phone. She finally got through to Audrey and relaxed when she told her Callie was with her but obviously didn't want to see her. Dillon might not be in love with Callie, but she didn't want anything bad to happen to her.

Bill had called on three separate occasions, inviting her and Callie to dinner or out on their boat, and Dillon had successfully declined the invitation for one reason or another. But if she didn't accept the next time, they would grow suspicious. Bill had already mentioned that Phyllis had been trying to get in touch with Callie for several days and she had not yet returned her call. Dillon couldn't remember what excuse she gave for that one.

She was still looking out the window when Greg came in. "Dillon?"

"Unless you have some good news to tell me about Callie, I don't want to hear it."

Greg had been on the receiving end of her wrath ever since Callie had stormed out of her office. He had also been her rock, practically running the company for her. She was distracted, had lost her focus, and couldn't remember where she was supposed to be and when. He kept her on schedule, made her sign what needed to be signed, and otherwise left her alone.

A few days after Callie learned about her deception Dillon went home and knew something was different the moment she let herself in through the garage door. It wasn't the fact that Callie's car was gone, but that the inside of her house felt empty, lifeless. She knew without looking that Callie had been there and collected her things. She didn't need to see the empty space on the mantel where the picture of Michael had been displayed or absence of the dozen or so books she had stacked next to the already bulging bookcase or the hangers hanging in the closet stripped of their contents to know that Callie was out of her life.

She roamed from room to room, noticing for the first time how lonely and desolate her house was—her life was. Callie brought few material things with her, but she had filled Dillon's house with energy. Every room came alive with Callie, even when she wasn't physically in it. The mere hint of her presence was all it took. But the condition of Callie's studio made Dillon feel like her guts had been laid open. Callie's painting supplies were gone, but she had left the works that depicted their life together. The canvases were piled haphazardly in a corner, discarded like their marriage.

Dillon's house was cold and empty, like a sarcophagus. Her bed was suddenly too big and she was sleeping in the guest bedroom— trying to sleep was more accurate. She hadn't managed more than three or fours hours a night for weeks.

She nodded at Greg's briefing, neither of them saying anything. She had bitten his head off more than once, and he was all business lately. The sadness around her pressed closer. Greg didn't deserve this treatment.

"Join me for coffee?" Dillon asked by way of an opening. Greg looked surprised but he recovered enough to get them both a cup. When he returned, Dillon motioned for him to sit on the couch with her.

"How are you holding up?" he asked tentatively.

"I could say great. I could say that I'm glad it's over and I can get on with my life. I could say that monogamy never really was my style. I could say a lot of things." Dillon held the cup and saucer with both hands to hide the fact that her hands were shaking.

"What do you want to say?"

"That I miss her," Dillon responded without hesitation. "That I didn't intend to treat her like this. That I'm sorry she ended up getting hurt. That someday she will find it in herself to forgive me. That I'm not stupid enough to believe she will."

Dillon had thought all of these things every day for the past several weeks. She had been profoundly affected by the pain she'd caused Callie. She had never before known that she had hurt someone so deeply or experienced this degree of agony and guilt over doing something.

"What do you plan to do?"

That was the number-one question Dillon had yet to find an answer for. She lay awake at night thinking about Callie and picturing her body in the shadows that danced on the dark ceiling. She listened for her voice, her laugh in the rustle of the leaves on a windy day. She looked for her wavy blond hair in crowds, coming up empty every time. Callie had filled her but now she was empty.

She didn't know when it happened. It's not like she woke up one day and said, "Today's the day I'm going to fall in love," and, poof, she did. But she *had* fallen in love with Callie. Somewhere between "Would you like to dance" and "I do," it happened. She knew now that she never would have married Callie if she hadn't been in love with her. She would have stopped the charade long before. Dillon was many things, but she drew the line at such an act. At least she did now.

Injuring Callie was like cutting out a piece of her own heart. She had wounded the woman she loved—whether intentionally or not didn't matter. Callie had been vulnerable and she had taken advantage of her situation. Not only the men who attacked her but the judicial system designed to punish the perpetrators had crushed her spirit. And now the woman who had promised to love, honor, and cherish her had victimized her yet again. Dillon had never actually said that she would protect Callie from being hurt again, but she knew Callie believed the vows they exchanged that summer day meant so much more than the words they uttered. Not only had she not protected Callie, she had caused her unpardonable pain, and Dillon had no idea how to heal it.

"I'd fall on my sword and beg her forgiveness, but I think she'd delight in twisting it in a little farther," Dillon finally answered. "Got any ideas? You've done this a few more times than I have." Greg had broken up and got back together with more girlfriends than Dillon could keep track of.

"Grovel. That's the key. Red-blooded American groveling. A little begging and pleading couldn't hurt either." He sipped his coffee and looked at Dillon before he spoke again. "Are you in love with her?"

"Yes," Dillon replied without having to think about it. "Yes, I am. It took her leaving for me to realize it. Jesus, where was Callie six months before I had to go to Bill's for that stupid dinner party?" Then all of this wouldn't be happening.

"You weren't ready for her," Greg said.

"You're right. I wasn't ready to settle down, and I certainly wasn't ready to fall in love. I wouldn't have recognized it if it had slapped me in the face. I probably would have slapped back and kept walking." Dillon rose from the couch, too restless to sit still for long.

"Isn't that what you did?"

Dillon stared at Greg. His words were the most profound thing she had ever heard. "Are you a shrink in your spare time?"

"Who has spare time? You keep me so busy I hardly have time to have a nice dinner with a beautiful woman, let alone anything else."

Dillon explored what Greg had said. Did she slap Callie away? Certainly not literally. She would never harm her physically, but figuratively? Did she keep her at bay by continuing the charade and not admitting that she had fallen in love with her? Callie loved her, that was evident, and even though Dillon had said the magic words to Callie, she thought at the time they were just words she needed to say.

But they were more than mere words and, like the marriage thing, she never would have said them unless she meant them somewhere down deep. Her feelings for Callie had been buried so far inside her that when she left, she ripped a hole in her soul with such force that Dillon couldn't help but finally see them.

"I don't know, Greg. She won't return my calls, she refuses my flowers. What makes me think she'll talk to me? She'll probably shoot me. Worse yet, say nothing and keep walking."

That was the most terrible thing that could happen. If Callie did shoot her, at least she would be out of her misery. But Callie not speaking to her ever again was crushing. She had to find a way. There had to be something that would prove to Callie that she was sorry any of this had happened and that she loved her for who she was, not for what she could get from her.

❖

"I did something really stupid."

Laura stared at Dillon like that was anything but a news flash. "Like what? Did you do something to break Callie's heart?"

"It didn't start out that way."

Laura's head shot up from her menu. Dillon realized Laura had spoken in jest and that she didn't expect Dillon's answer. Dillon had asked her to lunch to talk about what happened with Callie and to help her try to sort out her feelings.

"It never does."

"I need your help right now, Laura, not your attitude," Dillon snapped. Laura could be so judgmental at times, and by the looks of it, this was going to be one of those times.

"Let me hear what you did before you start assuming I'll help you," Laura said after their waiter had taken their order and left them alone.

Dillon told her the whole sordid story, leaving nothing out. She could never lie to her sister, and she saw her confession as taking responsibility for her actions. She had matured a lot in the past few weeks but realized she had a long way to go.

"Jesus, Dillon, how could you be so callous?" The disgust in her voice was obvious.

"I told you it didn't begin that way. I had no idea everything would spiral so far out of control," Dillon pleaded.

Laura barely let her finish. "Bullshit. Admit to yourself the scheme went exactly how you wanted it to."

"But I—"

"But nothing and don't interrupt. Not doing anything to stop it is the same as making it happen. You are responsible for this mess. Dillon, how could you? If this is the way you run your business you deserve to be married to *it*, not Callie."

Laura and Callie had grown close, so her reaction didn't surprise Dillon. "Don't worry, she doesn't want anything to do with me."

"Do you blame her?"

"No." She said the single word quietly.

"So, what do you want from me? The way I see it there's nothing I can do for you, even if I wanted to."

"Will you talk to her?"

"And say what? That my sister is an asshole, a pig, and a liar? I don't think Callie needs me to tell her that."

Laura's words stung, but they were nothing compared to the pain Dillon had inflicted on Callie.

Laura stood up. "You're my sister, Dillon, and I love you. I will always love you, but right now I have absolutely no respect for you."

She walked out of the room, leaving Dillon alone literally and figuratively. She had put herself in this position and she was the only one who could get herself out.

❖

Callie stood on the threshold, her hands shaking so hard she could barely push the doorbell. She started counting to one hundred to keep from turning and running down the steps, across the drive, and back into her car. The door opened and her heart stopped. Dillon stood in front of her in bare feet, wearing a dark blue pullover sweater and ragged blue jeans.

They stood there several minutes. At first glance Dillon looked the same, but as Callie studied her closer she could detect the deeply etched lines around her eyes and the pallor of her skin.

Finally Dillon spoke. "Callie." It was both a question and a statement.

"Hello, Dillon."

Dillon's eyes raked over her body from head to toe several times, as if she was trying to convince herself that Callie was actually standing in front of her. In spite of herself, Callie's body responded. Dillon knew every nook and cranny on it and definitely what to do once she got there. How could Callie not respond?

Dillon shook her head. "I'm sorry, please come in." She stepped back to give Callie room to pass.

Seeing Dillon, even after everything that had happened, Callie wanted to melt into her strong embrace. But she couldn't. Not after her betrayal. She had a plan and she had to stick to it. "No, not until we talk."

Dillon looked surprised at her statement. "All right." She stepped onto the porch and closed the door behind her. Though Dillon seemed anything but patient, she waited for Callie to speak.

"I have a proposition for you," Callie began, before she could lose her nerve. "I talked to Bill yesterday. He still thinks we're happily married, and I get the impression that he wouldn't be too pleased to learn the details of your little scheme."

Dillon flinched at the word "scheme," especially since Laura had used exactly the same word, but didn't do anything to stop Callie.

"You need me to close this deal and I need something from you. If you're looking for a business arrangement, I'll give it to you. In return for my continuing to pretend that we're madly in love, you will keep on funding Michael's appeal. That's it. No strings, nothing more than business. You get your project and Daddy's approval, and Michael gets out of jail. Then I'll walk away and no one will be the wiser about your dirty little secret."

Dillon was stunned. She had imagined many scenarios and what she would say if she was given the chance to talk to Callie again, but this was certainly not one she ever thought would happen. Callie was offering to trade herself for the resources to get her brother out of prison. Dillon fell in love with her all over again.

"Come on, Dillon, which is it, yes or no? I don't plan to wait here all day. I have things to do," Callie replied sternly, taking charge of the conversation and herself.

Dillon wanted Callie in her life, and if this was how it had to be, she would be a fool not to accept her offer. She knew their arrangement would be short-lived, but given the way she felt right now, it was better than nothing. She would worry about tomorrow later.

"Yes."

Callie's expression didn't change.

Since when was she so controlled? Since you ripped her heart out, stupid.

"Fine. I'll be back tomorrow morning." Callie started down the steps, then stopped and turned around. "Oh, and Dillon." She hesitated. "We consummated this marriage under false pretences. I won't make that mistake again. This is business, just business, as you phrased it, and I don't mix business with pleasure."

CHAPTER EIGHTEEN

Dillon watched Callie walk down the sidewalk. Other than when she made her parting condition, Callie never looked back, nor did she look at Dillon once she was safely inside her car. She simply turned on the ignition, backed out of the drive, and calmly drove down the street. Dillon stood there until the retreating taillights rounded the corner.

The silence echoed through the house louder than ever. Callie was coming back, filling every room with her physical presence, but things wouldn't be the same. Her body would be there but her soul would not. Dillon poured a drink and opened the patio door. The sun had set, leaving the sky coated with broad brushstrokes of reds and yellows.

The first star appeared and she recalled a familiar childhood chant as if it were yesterday.

> *Star light, star bright,*
> *The first star I see tonight,*
> *I wish I may, I wish I might,*
> *Have the wish I wish tonight.*

❖

Callie pulled into a crowded parking lot not far from Dillon's house. She had remained in control while in front of Dillon, but as soon as she parked and turned off the ignition, her hands began to shake and her stomach lunged into her throat. She fought back the urge to vomit and took several deep breaths. That didn't work so she simply sat cocooned in her car until the sensations passed.

When she finally looked up, it was dark. The lights were on in the parking lot, throwing harsh shadows all around her. She turned the key just enough for the clock to illuminate, telling her she had sat there for over an hour. This time she was calm as she thought about what she had just done, probably the calmest she had been since this charade was exposed. She controlled her life again. She was in charge and planned to stay that way.

Over the past few days she had done some research and discovered that the sale of Bill's land to Dillon was still in escrow, which meant that either party could pull out at any time and for any reason. The person who withdrew would incur a stiff penalty, but Dillon had a lot more to lose than Bill. Callie could do this, she would do this. She *had* to do this.

Last week when she'd gone to Lompak, Michael's appearance shocked her. He entered the visitation room with a large bandage across his forehead and ambled listlessly across the small room to the phone station. He looked twice at the hard stool and, after a moment of obviously weighing the alternatives, he gingerly sat down. His bottom lip was spilt and sewed together with black stitches, and his nose appeared to be broken, which would account for his two black eyes.

He refused to talk about what happened to him and even told Callie that if she mentioned it, he would leave and their visit would be over. She imagined what her brother must have had to endure to be as battered as he was. The way he had studied the stool, as if deciding if he could sit on it or not, had given her nightmares every night since.

On the long return drive from Lompak, Callie had made the decision that would affect the rest of her life. She had adamantly refused to consider Audrey's suggestion, but after seeing Michael she knew she didn't have another choice. She wrestled with her decision for days, and when Dillon opened the door, she almost changed her mind. Dillon still affected her in a way she didn't want her to. Her own body betrayed her. Intellectually she knew she should only feel anger and hatred toward Dillon, but her body craved Dillon's touch.

That craving continued and was even stronger when she saw Dillon again. Callie closed her eyes. The image of Dillon standing on the porch danced across her eyelids. Dillon's eyes were cautious, her expression weary, but she still had that same smoldering sensuality that drew Callie closer. Dillon didn't try to defend her unspeakable actions or excuse her behavior. She didn't beg or plead or get angry. She didn't attempt to say anything. She simply let Callie talk.

Callie had watched Dillon objectively as she contemplated her proposal. Dillon gazed at her as if she could see right through her and clearly weighed her options carefully before she answered. In one sense Dillon's decision didn't surprise her. If Dillon was the type of person who could go through with her plan secretly, she certainly wouldn't hesitate to continue now that it was out in the open. Callie had read her perfectly.

❖

The house smelled of pine oil and flowers when Callie opened the front door. It was Wednesday and she wasn't sure if Dillon would be here when she arrived. She didn't ring the bell. It was her house too, and she refused to be treated as if she were a guest. She planned to hold up her end of the bargain, and with it came all the privileges of being Mrs. Dillon Matthews.

Audrey had been surprised when Callie told her that she planned to return to the house. Even though she had originated the idea, she tried to talk her out of it. But Callie was firm, and eventually Audrey accepted her decision.

This time when she took her things into Dillon's house she put them in the guest bedroom at the top of the stairs. Dillon's bedroom, previously their bedroom, was at the end of the hall. The door was open and Callie had no interest in returning to the scene of that crime.

She put her clothes away and her toiletries in the adjoining bathroom. This room, like the others, had a king-size bed flanked by two nightstands, a headboard, dresser, and bureau. The cherrywood had recently been polished and gleamed in the midmorning sun. The architectural touches in this room were as unique as Dillon. The ceiling was vaulted, giving the impression that it was actually larger than it really was. The casings around the doors and windows were four inches wide and tied in with the crown molding high on the tan walls.

Several throw rugs covering the wood floor added a homey atmosphere, but she felt anything but at home. At one time she had embraced the massive residence as a sacred space, walking from room to room imagining what her life would be like living in such grandeur. Now she felt as bought and staged as the furnishings in the professionally decorated room.

A noise from Dillon's room drew her out into the hall just as Dillon herself emerged from it. Wearing a pair of khaki shorts, a blue polo shirt, and deck shoes, she stopped in the middle of the hall, as if she didn't expect to see Callie standing there.

"Callie."

She was momentarily unsettled because she hadn't had the opportunity to prepare herself for the onslaught of Dillon's raw sexuality. Her heart pounded and her mouth was suddenly dry. She squared her shoulders and recovered quickly.

"I told you I'd be back today."

Dillon seemed to recover from her surprise a little more slowly than Callie and tentatively stepped forward. "Yes, you did. I wasn't sure when, but I wanted to be here when you came home."

It unsettled Callie to hear Dillon say the word. It *had been* her home. She had tended to it, cared for it, and made love in every room of it. Dillon had made it a home, Callie's home. But now she preferred to think of it as only where she lived. She needed to maintain her distance from Dillon and all they shared at one time, and the best way was to depersonalize everything.

"You didn't need to be here."

Dillon walked toward her. "I wanted to." She had rescheduled her appointments, freeing the entire day to be with Callie. "I'll help you get the rest of your things," she said, and began to move toward the stairs.

"I don't need your help," Callie replied harshly. "I'm settled in and have to go to work. I'll be back around six thirty." Callie headed down the stairs.

"Callie, we have to talk," Dillon pleaded from the top of the stairs.

Callie turned and looked at her, impatience written all over her face.

"About us, this." Dillon put her palms up, indicating their surroundings.

She didn't know what she was supposed to do and not do. Callie had made it perfectly clear that they would not be sleeping together, but what about everything else? How was she supposed to act when they were in public together? Was she allowed to hold her hand as people would expect? Would they pretend they were still madly in love? Would they live under the same roof but maintain separate lives? Would they eat dinner together or was it every woman for herself? What level of roommates would they be?

"We do need to set some ground rules, Dillon. We'll talk about it tonight."

With that, Callie strode across the foyer and out the door, for the second time in as many days leaving Dillon staring at her receding back. Dillon stayed where she was until she heard Callie's car start and drive away. She sat down on the top step and put her head in her hands. How could she have been so stupid? She wanted to be here to welcome Callie home, and she was dumb enough to think that her presence mattered. Callie didn't want to be in her home, let alone welcomed as if nothing had happened.

Dillon toyed with the idea of still taking the day off. Maybe she'd go to the marina, perhaps play a round of golf or sit out by the pool and read one of the books she'd ordered last week. Seeing Callie again in her house was nerve-racking enough, and she wouldn't be able to concentrate on anything that demanded her full attention.

She stood, fully intending to retrace her steps to her bedroom, but stopped just outside the door to Callie's room. It was closed, and

Dillon would be invading her privacy if she went inside. As much as she wanted to see that Callie had actually moved back in, that her brush was on the counter, her shoes lined up neatly on the closet floor, Dillon couldn't do it. She had screwed up enough and didn't want to risk doing anything to add ammunition to Callie's hatred of her. Frowning, she continued down the hall.

❖

Audrey met Callie for lunch at the park not far from the flower shop, and they had barely sat down at a table before Audrey peppered her with questions.

Callie held up her hands in surrender. "Okay, okay, give me a minute and I'll tell you." She had refused Audrey's offer to go with her when she took her things back to Dillon's, preferring to face her demons alone. She would have to sooner or later, so she opted for sooner.

She popped open her Cherry Coke can and took a big swig, preparing for Audrey's twenty questions. Even if there was nothing to say, Audrey would still have twenty questions.

"I took my stuff over this morning."

"Was she there?"

"Yes. She took the day off to be there. I don't know why. It's not as if I was moving in for the sheer pleasure of living with her. For God's sake, did she actually think I wanted to see her?" Callie tore open her bag of Cheetos with such force, bright orange curlicues flew everywhere.

"What did she say? How did she look?"

Callie sighed. Three down, seventeen more to go. "She didn't say much, I didn't say much. She said we had to talk, and because I was late for work, I told her we would tonight. I jetted out the door before she could get another word in. That's it." Callie made light of the scene, but she imagined it was only round one.

"Did you put your things in the guest room?" Callie had told Audrey the terms of the arrangement and that sleeping with Dillon was definitely not one of them. "Did she say anything about that?"

"We didn't talk about much, Audrey. She knows I'm not going to sleep with her. Where else would I put my clothes? I'm certainly not going to put them in her closet if I'm sleeping in the room down the hall." Callie's temper was understandably short today.

"Are you sure you can go through with this, Callie? I mean, you really loved her and she majorly shit on you. I'm worried about you." The concern in Audrey's voice was sincere.

"I know you care, Audrey, but I can do this. Remember how we were in the play *Oklahoma* in high school? This is just like that. I'll pretend I'm someone else. As a matter of fact, I can probably do it with my eyes closed. After all, I've learned from the best, haven't I? If Dillon can fake it, so can I." Callie wished it were only going to be that easy.

❖

Later that evening Dillon walked into the kitchen wearing the suit Callie had told her was her favorite, a gray Chanel pinstripe with a darker gray blouse. The suit set off the color of her eyes, making her look powerful and professional, yet the silk shell under the perfectly tailored jacket added a touch of femininity. Dillon was pulling off the jacket and stopped when she saw her.

"I thought you were off today." Callie's pulse raced at how sexy Dillon looked in her power clothes. She was disgusted with herself for reacting like that. Callie hadn't even been sure Dillon would be coming home, and here she was already beginning to admire Dillon's appearance.

"Obviously there was no reason for me to be here all day. Greg is on vacation, and the place goes to hell if at least one of us isn't there."

The smell of spaghetti sauce filled the air, and for the first time since Callie left, Dillon was actually hungry. She wondered if the fact that Callie was cooking dinner was a good sign. She hadn't had a chance to think about that possibility when Callie told her dinner was almost ready and for her to change her clothes and come right back.

Dillon practically flew up the steps and raced down the hall, unbuttoning her pants and pulling her blouse over her head before she reached her room. She didn't want to miss a minute that she could be with Callie. She pulled on a pair of shorts and a green tank top and glanced in the mirror. Her hair was a mess and her face was flushed from the exertion. She ran her fingers through her dark hair and took the steps down two at a time. Her feet landed hard at the base of the stairs and she slid into the dining room just as Callie was setting the bowl of spaghetti on the table with one hand, the pot of sauce in the other.

"Here, let me help you," she offered, taking the pot from her and placing it on the warming cloth. "Is there anything else, anything you want me to do?" Dillon didn't want Callie to think she had to wait on her as payment for Michael's defense.

"No, that's everything." Callie sat across the table from Dillon instead of to her right, as she had before.

"It smells wonderful," Dillon commented, piling spaghetti on her plate.

"Thanks. It's quick and easy, and I didn't get home much before you did. I got held up in traffic."

So far, so good, Dillon thought. *We're having a normal conversation, that's good. Safe topics—the meal, the traffic. That's good too. Maybe next we'll talk about the chance of rain tomorrow or how much snow Lake Tahoe got this year.*

But actually they didn't talk about anything. They ate in almost complete silence, with only the clinking of silverware on plates breaking the loudest sound in the world.

When dinner was finally over, Dillon gathered up the dishes. Callie had always teased her that the cook never does the dishes, and she had gotten into the habit of taking care of them each evening she was home for dinner. If Callie had gone to the trouble to make dinner, Dillon could at least clean up.

She dawdled in the kitchen as long as she reasonably could before she joined Callie on the back patio. She hadn't been invited and wasn't sure she would even be welcome, but she wanted to be with Callie. They had to establish some sort of routine or she wouldn't able to cope.

"May I join you?"

"It's your house." Callie didn't look at Dillon.

She let the caustic comment slide. She didn't want to get into an argument on Callie's first evening back.

"Dinner was delicious, thank you." More benign chatter.

Dillon had never felt so verbally impotent as she had since Callie moved back in. They used to talk about everything and nothing, their silences comfortable and full. Now silence hung in the air like the proverbial elephant in the room, the tension so thick it was suffocating.

"You said you wanted to talk," Callie said.

Dillon's stomach jumped and she was suddenly nervous. She had never been in this position before with a woman. Someone else was calling the shots, determining what she would do next. Other than Bill's holdout on the land purchase she couldn't remember the last time she wasn't in complete control. She didn't know what to do.

"Obviously we're not your typical loving, married couple anymore—"

"We never were."

Ouch. "Point taken. We need to lay some ground rules. About our behavior," Dillon added carefully.

"Our behavior?" Callie couldn't believe they were even talking about this. Callie's anger snapped. "And what behavior is that, Dillon? When you lied to me? When you used me? Or the dozens of times you fucked me to get what you wanted?" She had no idea her rage was sitting this close to the surface. She had expected it to surface a day or two after she found out, not now.

Dillon leaned back as if she had been slapped, and though she recoiled, she weakly defended herself. "It wasn't like that, Callie."

"And just how was it, Dillon? Tell me, hmm? No, wait, I think I can fill in the pieces. You needed Bill's land to prove something to your father and he wouldn't sell it to you. You needed a relationship, something to show Bill there was more to you than business. Better yet, a wife. You find me sitting alone in a bar nursing a beer and feeling sorry for myself, and you come in on your white horse and save me from myself. You sweep me off my feet, promising to love, honor, and cherish. Oh, and let's not forget the little matter of paying for Michael's defense lawyer. That was brilliant. You knew just how to get to me. You knew just how to get me to fall in—"

Callie caught herself just in time. She would not be humiliated again by declaring her love for Dillon. "You had it all figured out. You got both the land and the right to sleep with the girl. Quite a coup, Dillon, I'll give you that." Callie sat back in her chair.

"Do I get a chance to say anything?" Callie hadn't taken a breath during her tirade, and even though Dillon hoped it was over, she doubted it was. Dillon took advantage of Callie's silence. "You're right. About everything. You even got it in the right order. But you missed a couple of things. First, I saw you at the bar and was attracted to you, and I will admit that my first thought was to take you home, but I didn't. Give me some credit for a little self-respect. Second, I did not see you as a meal ticket to Bill's land."

Dillon stopped. She had just said what she knew Callie wanted to hear. In the past she had said plenty of things she didn't mean to other women. She had also said things she didn't want to close deals. She was the master negotiator, and if she wanted, she could choose to treat this relationship like any other deal. But this time she couldn't. This was Callie and she was in love with her. Even if Callie could never love her, she had to make amends.

She took a deep breath. "At least not at first. I liked you. You were genuine, which was something I hadn't seen in a woman in a long time. You seemed innocent, and other than Michael's situation, you weren't jaded by the world yet. And speaking of Michael, I don't want to see anyone who has been wrongfully convicted in jail." Dillon downed several swallows from her bottle of water. "I didn't fuck you, Callie. I never thought that making love with you was payment in kind for anything, nor did I think it was my right to have you. Did it bring you closer to me? Yes, it did, but it also brought me closer to you. I know you'll probably never believe this,

Callie, but I wanted to make love to you because I desired *you*. Not because I expected you to perform some conjugal duty."

At this point Dillon was tempted to get down on her knees and beg for forgiveness, to tell Callie how much she meant to her. That she had fallen in love with her and was miserable without her. That she would cut off her arm to make the pain of deceit go away. That she wanted Callie to marry her for real this time.

But Callie would never believe her. No matter what she said she wouldn't believe a word of it. But Dillon did have the opportunity to try to make things right. She would beg and grovel and plead the only way she knew how—by showing Callie how very much she loved her.

"Callie, why are you here?"

"I'm here because my brother was beaten and raped while in prison for a crime he didn't commit, and I need money to get him out. That's the only reason. I don't care about you or your stupid little project or your misguided lack of self-worth with your father. I will sell my soul to the devil to get Michael out of prison, and if you're her, then so be it."

Callie stared at her as if she were a stranger on a street corner. "When we're out in public we will act like we're in love, maintain the typical relationship that married couples do. You can hold my hand and gaze longingly into my eyes, but let me make this perfectly clear, Dillon. You can have my body and the pretense of a happy marriage, but you will never have me. Never again."

Chapter Nineteen

One evening two weeks after Callie returned home Dillon said, "Bill called today. He wanted to know when we can get together again for dinner."

Callie seemed to shudder when Dillon mentioned Bill's name. "What did you tell him?"

"That you hold the social calendar and I'd have to talk to you." Callie held more than their social calendar. She held all the cards, and for now that was okay with Dillon.

"What do you want to do?"

"In spite of this whole thing, I like them. They're great people without a mean bone between them and fun to be with," Dillon replied hesitantly. Previously, Callie had enjoyed spending time with them, but Dillon didn't know what she thought of them now. They weren't to blame for what had happened, and she needed to clarify that point.

"Callie, Bill and Phyllis had nothing to do with this. Bill and I never discussed this situation, and it was never a condition of him selling me his property. I saw it as an opportunity to exploit what I thought I needed to do to get what I wanted. Nothing more. Don't take out your hatred for me on them."

"Thank you for clearing that up."

Callie had wondered how much involvement Bill and Phyllis had in their marriage. They had become more than a little involved in the preparation of the wedding and their life together, but they were a sweet couple who seemed to want to see others as happy as they were. Dillon's admission was surprising. She very easily could have portrayed them as willing accomplices, but she didn't. She accepted full responsibility.

This wasn't the first time, either. A week earlier she had taken the full brunt of another of Callie's explosions as they were driving back from Lompak. Dillon had made an innocent comment about Michael's defense lawyer, and Callie had exploded. She didn't remember exactly what Dillon had said, but Dillon had sat quietly while she lashed out at her.

"I miss them," Callie admitted. "I'd like to see them again."

"You know what they'll expect to see, don't you? I don't want either of us to misunderstand our roles. And I certainly don't want you to be uncomfortable or embarrassed."

"Don't worry, your secret is safe with me. I would never do anything to jeopardize Michael's defense."

Callie was surprised at her reaction. One minute she recognized Dillon's assumption of responsibility, and the next she snapped at her. She hated the way she was acting, but she couldn't help herself.

Dillon didn't snap back, although she could have said that she didn't need to be reminded of the arrangement. Instead she said, "I didn't think you would. I was only concerned for you. You know how Bill and Phyllis are. I truly don't want our socializing with them to be awkward or difficult for you."

Callie wanted to apologize for jumping to conclusions, but she couldn't get the words out of her mouth. Instead she softened her next ones. "I appreciate that. I know what they expect to see—the way we were the last time we were all together. I can do it. They won't have a clue we're anything but deeply in love."

This would be the first real challenge of their newly negotiated peace, and she wondered if she really could pull it off without Dillon realizing how much she still affected her. If she actually detested Dillon's touch, she would be able to remain internally distant. She wouldn't have to hide her reaction to how Dillon's skin felt when she touched it. How it jumped when she caressed it, how she could feel the heat grow under her fingertips. Dillon could never know. That was her trump card.

❖

Callie was nervous as they waited for the Franklins to open their front door. She had spent far too long in her closet choosing something to wear. It should have been easy—a pair of slacks or a sundress—but it wasn't. She felt as if she was going to be on display and she needed all of her armor in place. She had settled for a simple blue dress with capped sleeves and sandals and rubbed her arms as the seconds ticked by.

"Cold?"

Callie dropped her hands. "Just a chill. I'm fine."

Dillon took a deep breath. "You look very nice."

Before they left their house, Dillon had obviously been waiting for Callie in the living room, and she'd stared when Callie came down the stairs. Her dress swirled around her knees and she had pulled her hair back, so Dillon was looking at her neck. She had decided to carry a light sweater, in case it got cool later, and when she grabbed her purse from the side table, they were ready to go. Dillon's stare made Callie feel uneasy.

And just now, when Dillon complimented her, Callie looked at her suspiciously.

Dillon seemed on the verge of losing her temper, but shook her head and merely said, "What? I said you looked nice, that's all. No ulterior motive, no hidden agenda. Just a simple compliment, and a simple thank you would be nice."

Callie felt foolish. Since she had moved back, Dillon had done everything she expected her to do to hold up her end of the bargain and hadn't given her any reason to doubt her—that she knew of. But that was the problem. Callie didn't trust her. Why should she? She started to say thank you but the opening of the front door saved her.

"Well, it's about time," Bill bellowed, a big grin on his face.

"We thought you two had disappeared behind closed doors and would never come out. But if I had a girl like you do, Dillon, I wouldn't want to come out either." Bill winked at Dillon.

Callie slid her hand into Dillon's. "Actually, Bill, it's the other way around." She stepped forward to kiss him on the cheek. Phyllis was coming up behind him, wiping her hands on a dish towel.

Greetings completed, they all settled on the back porch with Bill playing the role of bartender. Callie sat in close proximity to Dillon, her body constantly reminding her just how close.

"So, Callie, is married life everything you thought it would be?" Phyllis set a tray of crackers and cheese on the table in front of them.

"Actually, Phyllis, it's a lot more than I expected." Dillon tensed beside her.

"Oh, how so?"

"Well, I underestimated just how intertwined our lives would be, how dependent we would be on each other. I need things that only Dillon can give me, and I don't want to speak for her, but I think it's the same with Dillon. I'm committed to this marriage as much as Dillon is." Callie moved her hand to Dillon's thigh and her leg jumped at the contact.

"Dillon?" Phyllis asked.

Dillon covered Callie's hand with her own. "I've definitely learned that my wife is smart, very smart, and I respect her tremendously. We're in this for the long haul, and if I'd known it would be like this, I would have tracked her down and married her years ago."

Dillon squeezed Callie's hand, and Callie wondered what she meant. Did she actually respect her now, or were these simply more of her lies? She certainly hadn't respected her before now.

After dinner Phyllis mentioned that she had some pictures of the wedding that she didn't think Dillon and Callie had seen. She loaded them on her laptop and projected them onto the wall before Callie could change the subject. As Phyllis flipped through the images of the wedding, bittersweet memories swept over Callie as she was seemingly transported back to the actual day.

The love she felt for Dillon as she walked down the aisle had overwhelmed her then. She was totally in love—strong and powerful, her confidence spilling over into everything she was. She was in love and was loved in return. Or at least she thought she was.

Image after image danced across the wall as if they were snapshots of her life, the only part of her life that really mattered. Callie had divided her relationship with Dillon into two parts— before she found out about the deception and after. Seeing these glimpses of the "before," she was tempted to downplay the "after." But she couldn't do that to herself. She had to see things as they actually were.

Some pictures of the ceremony showed Dillon standing at the altar looking striking in her Armani tuxedo. Her eyes sparkled and she looked just a bit scared. Their first kiss was captured, quickly followed by their first dance. In shot after shot Dillon gazed at her as if she really was in love with her. But Callie knew better now. As she viewed the photos, she felt rather than saw Dillon looking at her and fought against returning the gaze. Mercifully the last picture closed.

Callie was a little buzzed from the wine she had consumed to get through the slide show and on the way home asked, "Did you have a good time?"

"Yes, I did. How about you?"

Callie didn't answer the question directly. "You were right. They are wonderful people. My heart hurts when I think about the tragedy with Haley. Terrible things like that shouldn't happen to anyone, let alone to people as kind as they are." She couldn't even imagine what they must have felt when they heard the news about their granddaughter.

Dillon said, "I never knew my grandparents. They all died when I was young. Even if they had lived, I could only hope they would love me regardless of who I loved." *Unlike my father* went unspoken.

"I don't know if mine are alive or dead. I suppose I could track them down, but then again, they could do the same. I doubt that my father's parents even know they have grandchildren or, I should say, about me and Michael. God knows who else is out there as a result of my father."

"Do you get the feeling that Bill and Phyllis consider us their surrogate granddaughters?" Dillon asked the question that had plagued her the entire evening.

"Yes, I do, and I'm flattered."

Dillon didn't feel flattered. She felt guilty. She was a cad for deceiving Callie, and to exploit that deception with Bill and Phyllis was just as bad. They were good people with no ulterior motives. They didn't deserve to be treated the way she had done. What had she been thinking? They had been duped as much as Callie, and she was responsible for deceiving them. Shame covered her every day and she didn't know what to do to make it right. She said as much to Callie as she pulled into the drive and waited as the garage door opened.

"I feel a sense of responsibility to them."

Assuming responsibility for another person was a new feeling for Dillon. She rarely felt responsible for her family, let alone someone else. And some days she didn't even want to be responsible for herself. It was an odd, uncomfortable feeling.

She thought back to what she had told the Franklins earlier about Callie and their marriage. She did respect Callie, more than she had ever respected a woman. In the long nights when she lay awake longing for Callie she realized that she had treated a lot of women badly. Some had wanted more from her than she wanted to give, and she had brushed them off without considering their feelings at all. She didn't return phone calls and, when forced to give her number, she made one up.

Laura was right, she was a pig. It took falling in love with the right woman for her to realize it.

Chapter Twenty

The bell over the door chimed, and Callie glanced up from the flowers she was arranging. She had been thinking about the Franklins and the night she and Dillon spent with them. She hadn't realized how much she missed them until she saw them again. Also, spending the evening with Dillon wasn't as stressful as she thought it would be. They fell into a natural intimacy that came only with people who were together for a while. The history between them hadn't dampened that natural, comfortable chemistry. At the same time, she understood how dangerous her "marriage" with Dillon could be.

Callie held pink roses that she was inserting between white daisy poms. Her breath caught in her throat when Dillon walked in. It had been almost two weeks since their dinner with the Franklins, and Dillon had been home only four evenings since then.

Dillon had returned from her office one evening and informed her that she had to go out of town for a few days. As she headed upstairs to pack, she mumbled something about an issue on one of her projects. A few days turned into many more, and as of this morning when Callie left for work, Dillon was not back yet.

Callie drank in the image of Dillon. She wore dark gray silk trousers, a thin black belt, and a pristine white shirt barely visible under her light overcoat, giving her an androgynous look, and Callie's mouth went dry. Her naturally gray eyes seemed piercing black, and the dimples on her cheek stood out against her smile. She looked tired, yet she exuded a subtle sensuality that Callie couldn't help but respond to. Like with the Franklins, she didn't realize how much she had missed Dillon until she saw her again.

"Hi," Dillon said, walking toward the counter. "I hope I'm not interrupting anything." She glanced around the shop.

"You're back." Callie's pulse was racing.

"I got in this morning."

"How was your trip?" Dillon's close proximity and her long absence were making it hard to concentrate.

"You know, just business."

There was a long pause, and Callie jumped when Ross bellowed from behind her, "Well, look what the cat dragged in. How are you, Dillon?"

Dillon reached for the hand Ross extended. "I'm good, Ross. How are you?"

"No complaints. Where've you been? Callie hardly talks about you. Not like she did when you two were courting. I couldn't shut her up."

Dillon and Callie exchanged a cautious glance. "I've been out of town for a few days."

"Come to take your beautiful bride to lunch?" Ross asked.

Dillon looked at Callie. The expression on her face was almost unreadable, but Dillon knew her well enough to see that she had caught Callie off guard. When her plane landed this morning she had an overwhelming urge to see Callie. While she was gone she had managed to keep hold of her emotions and not act like a love-struck idiot, but as soon as she knew Callie was within touching distance she couldn't control them any longer.

The night they returned from the Franklins', Dillon had to force herself not to go to Callie's room. The evening had been difficult because they had acted as if they were still in love. Dillon wasn't acting, and every time Callie touched her or looked at her, her skin burned. She wanted Callie so badly she paced her room all night.

Normally when Dillon couldn't sleep, she swam laps in the pool until she was exhausted. But she didn't dare pass Callie's bedroom door half dressed, because she wouldn't be able to simply walk by. She paced from one side of the room to the other instead. At one time she began to count steps, and when she reached one thousand, she made herself stop counting.

She went to work that morning tired and on edge, and after the third time she barked at Greg, he left her alone for the remainder of the day. In the middle of the afternoon she told him to make arrangements for her to visit her three sites in Canada. One office complex was almost complete and the other two had recently broken ground. She had a new project manager on the largest of the two and wanted to keep a close eye on how the construction was going. Greg didn't sound surprised when she extended her trip an additional six days.

Typically when she traveled, she savored the nightlife and experienced the local delights if the right woman came along. But not this trip. She worked as much as she could, walked as far as she could go, and drank as much as her body would allow—and she still couldn't get Callie out of her mind. Everywhere she went she saw someone or something that reminded her of the woman who unknowingly held her heart in the palm of her hand. More than once she almost bought something she knew Callie would like, and she did buy a sapphire necklace that she planned to hold on to just in case she found an opportunity to give it to her.

The pounding of the music at the bar in Montreal had annoyed her more than energized her. She always found the women in that city attractive and exciting, but during this trip they seemed plain and dull. Several approached her in subtle and not-so-subtle ways, and she politely told them she wasn't interested. After a couple of hours she returned to the hotel alone.

She wanted to go home, but didn't dare until she got her emotions under control. She was consumed with images and thoughts of Callie. The first time they met, the first time they danced, the first cup of coffee they drank together. She could practically recite every conversation they had. The memories of their lovemaking were the strongest and most gut-wrenching. Callie's touch seemed to have burned itself into her flesh. She ached for her touch and her kisses. Only Callie could soothe the fire growing inside her.

Dillon had never felt as out of sorts as she had lately. She couldn't concentrate, was easily distracted, and had no appetite. Everything she ate tasted like chalk, and when she was forced to dine with a business associate, she usually pushed enough food around her plate to make it appear she had eaten.

So she had stayed away longer than she wanted and, judging by her reaction to Callie, not as long as she needed to.

But Dillon saw nothing in the room except Callie. The flowers were pale in comparison to the woman she had made her wife. Callie's blond hair was tucked behind one ear, a diamond earring winking at her. Her jeans accentuated her long legs, and Dillon halted her gaze at the rise and fall of her breasts. Callie seemed to breathe faster, and Dillon noticed her nipples harden under her T-shirt. It was all she could do to stay where she was.

"Or are you two just going to ravish each other right here on the counter?"

Dillon's subconscious registered Ross's voice. "I'm sorry, what did you say?"

"I asked if you came to take your lovely wife to lunch."

This time when Dillon looked at Callie she was prepared, or at least as prepared as she could be. "If she'll have lunch with me?" Dillon said as more of a question than a statement. A flicker of something flashed in Callie's eyes.

"Of course she will," Ross interjected. "Go on, you two, take as much time as you'd like. Far be it from me to stand between two women in love." The phone rang and Ross stepped over to answer it.

Dillon looked at Callie and wanted to say, "What are we supposed to do?"

Callie set the flowers she was still holding back in the cooler and grabbed her purse from under the counter and her jacket from the hook by the door. They didn't speak until they stepped outside.

"I'm sorry about that," Callie said as the brisk fall wind blew her hair into her face.

"About what?" Dillon asked, inhaling the clean scent of Callie.

It was the closest they had been to one another since dinner with the Franklins.

"What Ross said. We don't have to go to lunch. I can run a few errands instead."

"Actually, that's why I came by. We need to catch up, and keeping up appearances with Ross is part of our plan, isn't it? You haven't told him, have you?" Dillon didn't think Callie would purposefully embarrass herself by telling her friends about their arrangement, but she didn't want to assume anything.

"No, though I'm surprised you care. I expected you to be concerned only about what people think about the infamous Dillon Matthews."

Dillon winced. "So what about lunch? We have to eat and it *is* almost noon." She asked meekly, hoping Callie would say yes. She wanted to be with her—simply to look at her, listen to her voice, smell her hair. God, she had it bad. She was turning into a sappy version of herself, a lovesick puppy. But wasn't she?

"All right, though I'm not sure this is a good idea. But you do have a point. And we probably should catch up."

Dillon relaxed a little. At least she hadn't told her to go to hell. They walked across the street to the Italian restaurant they both loved. When they stepped inside, Dillon was suddenly ravenous. The smell of fresh-baked garlic bread assaulted her senses, and her stomach let out a loud growl of protest. Callie looked at first her stomach, then her face.

"Sorry. Guess I'm hungrier than I thought."

The hostess led them to a quiet table by the window, and before too long Dillon had a plate of lasagna in front of her while Callie nibbled on a Caesar salad. Dillon declined the waitress's suggestion for a glass of wine. She wanted to be sharp. She wanted to take in every detail of her lunch with Callie. She might have to rely on it for her "Callie fix" for a long time.

"How was your trip? Did you accomplish everything you needed to?" Callie sounded distant, barely interested, as if small talk was the only type of conversation that was bearable. But at least she asked something.

Dillon wanted to say no. *No, I couldn't get you out of my mind. No, I couldn't erase the memories of the way your body felt under me. I didn't get you out of my heart.*

"It was about what I expected," she replied instead. That wasn't a lie. Dillon had gone away because she didn't trust herself to be near Callie.

Dinner at the Franklins' had been torturous, and by the time they pulled into the driveway she thought she would jump out of her skin. Even though she knew Callie was acting, her body couldn't help but react to the way she looked at her and touched her. If Dillon didn't know better, she would have said that some of Callie's touches lingered a little longer than necessary to convince Bill and Phyllis that they were in love.

But she did know better. Callie hated her—and for good reason. She had used Callie for her own benefit without regard to her feelings, and Callie would never forgive her. Dillon had accepted that fact, but what she couldn't handle was the way she wanted her.

Dillon had fallen crazy in love with Callie. She had no idea when it happened or how, but she was absolutely, undeniably in love. During her time away Dillon had tried to analyze exactly how she knew this. She had never been in love before, so she had no real point of reference. But she did know that Callie was in her veins, in every pore and cell of her body. She was a part of her, and Dillon felt less than whole without her.

She had gone away on the fake pretense of a business trip to try to purge Callie from her system. She had visited her old haunts where the feel of a woman and hot breath on her skin made her forget everything except the moment. But she hadn't been the slightest bit interested in the scene around her. Another woman wouldn't purge Callie from her skin and so she didn't even try.

"Everything okay here?" Dillon added.

"Yes." *Everything except for the fact that you weren't.* "Laura called yesterday. Tim's birthday is in a couple of weeks, and she invited us to a party for him at their house."

Dillon managed to swallow another bite of lunch. She suspected her lasagna was delicious but her throat was too dry to enjoy it. "Did she say anything else?"

"Should she have?"

Dillon surmised that Laura was surprised when Callie answered the phone. She had probably covered her amazement by talking about Tim's party. But Dillon couldn't hide her own feelings that easily, though she tried by not answering Callie's question.

Callie asked another one. "You *told* her?"

Dillon was afraid to look at her. "She's my sister, and probably my only friend. I needed someone to talk to."

"So now she knows what a fool I am. Does anyone else know?"

"No," Dillon said quickly as Callie's words hit her in the stomach. Obviously she had hurt Callie again. Jesus, would she ever learn? "Nobody. Just Laura. She doesn't think you're a fool." Dillon gave up trying to eat and set her fork down. "She called me a pig." She glanced at Callie. "Actually she said I was an asshole, a pig, and a liar." Laura's words still stung, and because they were the truth they always would.

"I knew I liked her." Callie smiled. "She welcomed me into the family and was beginning to seem like the sister I never had, before…you know."

"I'm sorry. I'm sorry for all of this. I was selfish, self-centered, a pig, a cad, a liar, and everything else you want to call it. Probably even a few things I've never even heard of." Dillon looked Callie directly in the eye. "But I deserve all those names. I absolutely deserve them. I was all of those things and I am sorry. I am truly sorry. I hurt you and I will never forgive myself and I don't expect you to either. I used Bill and the loss of his granddaughter to get what I wanted. What I did was uncalled for, and nobody deserved to be treated the way I treated them. You especially. I played to your weakness and I can't tell you how sorry I am. I know you don't believe me, but if it takes me the rest of my life I'm going to try to make it up to you."

Callie looked stunned by Dillon's admission, and the lines

around her mouth softened, almost as if she wanted to believe it. But then the lines tightened again, and Dillon knew she had hurt Callie so deeply she would never accept anything she said.

"You're right, Dillon. We didn't deserve it." Callie wasn't going to let her off the hook.

"I've been thinking about coming clean with Bill and Phyllis." Dillon felt like she was in the middle of rehab, the phase where you confess your sins and ask for forgiveness. It was an uncomfortable place to be.

"Don't you dare." Callie's words were harsh. "Don't you hurt them too. Knowing what you did would devastate them."

Just like I did to you, Dillon thought. "All right, if you say so." Dillon let Callie make the call on this one. She would let her make the call on everything if she would only forgive her. On the way back from Canada, Dillon decided that she wanted Callie in her life and would do anything to get her back. It wouldn't be easy—it might be impossible—but she planned to try. She had to.

"Yes, I do. Telling them won't accomplish anything other than to ease your guilt. It would crush them, and I care too much for them to let that happen."

"I was just thinking about you."

"How so?"

"You're the one who has to put on an act whenever we're together. I was only trying to make it easier for you."

"At the expense of someone else?"

"No, not at all." The conversation was rapidly going downhill. "I was just…" Dillon sighed and dropped her head in her hands. "I don't know what to think anymore."

Dillon's confusion tore at the edges of Callie's heart. She didn't want to see her in pain, but it was the only way she would learn. She had to be held accountable for what she had done. This was more than just a business deal; she had fucked with people's lives. She had crossed the line.

"I know what you're trying to do and I appreciate it, Dillon, but I will decide what I have to do."

"All right. You're running the show here, you call the shots."

Callie knew she should feel better, superior, in charge, but she didn't. The selfish part of her, her pride, wanted to, but she couldn't. She didn't want to be morally better than Dillon. She wanted to be her equal. "Dillon—" She started to say as much, but Dillon interrupted her.

"It's getting late. You probably need to get back." She signaled for the check, effectively ending their conversation.

❖

When Dillon arrived back at her office, Greg was on the phone and motioned that the call was for her. She shook her head, not feeling up to dealing with anything, but when Greg informed her it was Michael, she hurried inside her office and picked up the receiver.

"Michael?" Callie had mentioned that even though her brother could make collect telephone calls, he never called her. Now here he was phoning Dillon. Her senses were on high alert.

"Dillon? I hope I'm not disturbing you."

Michael sounded like he was talking inside a cave. Dillon guessed he was in a room with more concrete than carpet.

"No, of course not, Michael. You can call anytime. Are you all right?"

"Yes, I'm fine. I just wanted to talk to you without Callie around."

"Okay." Dillon didn't know what else to say. During her visits to Lompak with Callie she had never really spoken with him. Callie was there to visit her brother and they did all of the talking. Dillon sat down in her chair, her eyes straying to the painting of the beach that Callie had given her on their wedding day. Next to it was a scene of a mountain lake.

"Dillon, I…uh…" he stopped. Obviously Michael was struggling with what he wanted to say.

She helped him out. "Michael, this conversation is between you and me. You're Callie's brother, and if you need something I'll do whatever I can to help you."

Dillon thought she heard him take a deep breath. "I want to thank you for what you're doing. For helping me. Paying for my attorney, Mr. Nixon." His sentences were coming out in short bursts. "I really appreciate it. You don't have to, you know."

"Michael, you don't have to thank me. I want to." Dillon did want to help Michael. She knew him only from what Callie had told her, and other than his current circumstances, he seemed to be a great guy.

"Yes, Dillon, I do. It means a lot to me." He paused as if deciding to say something else. "You know my sister really loves you."

Dillon heard a beep in her ear, reminding her that their conversation was being recorded. "How do you know?"

"The way she looks at you, the way her face lights up when she talks about you. Jesus, even the way she walks next to you when you two come into the room. She's got it bad." He chuckled.

The anonymity of the phone gave Dillon courage. "I love her too. Your sister is a wonderful woman." Dillon thought it was unusual that the first person she honestly declared her love for Callie to was a man locked up in a maximum-security prison.

"Yes, she is, and I don't want to see her get hurt."

Dillon didn't like the way the conversation had turned. "What makes you say that?"

"Because she's so head over heels in love with you, she's vulnerable."

"I have no intention of hurting her, Michael." *Any more than I already have.*

"I'm glad to hear that because I love her, and I don't know how much more shit in her life she can take."

Dillon breathed a little calmer. "I love your sister, Michael, and I'll do anything for her." Dillon's words echoed in her brain.

They exchanged a few more pleasantries and quickly ended the call. She dropped the receiver back into the cradle and suddenly felt exhausted.

❖

Their conversation nagged at Callie for the remainder of the day. She faced a barrage of questions from Ross when she returned from lunch, including one that said she didn't look like she had just come back from lunch with her new wife. She made up some excuse and did her best to avoid him the rest of the afternoon. On her way home she finally realized why their conversation had unsettled her so much.

Dillon had practically rolled over and played dead. She didn't defend herself or try to explain, and she definitely didn't make any excuses for what she had done. Would Dillon have assumed responsibility for World War II if she had accused her of it? She let Callie have anything, including the right to chew her butt over and over again if she wanted to.

Callie frowned as she pulled into the driveway. Did she have that much control over Dillon? Did she want that kind of power over another person? Over Dillon?

Parking her car, Callie turned off the engine and sat in the dim light of the garage. For so long she had barely held on to what she had, and now her entire world had changed. She had gone from practically nothing to having everything to back to practically nothing again. Sure, she had Dillon's name, her money, and the opportunities that came with this new position, but she was alone. She was living a shell of a life. A very beautiful shell but a shell nonetheless. Her life was empty. She was suddenly very tired.

She sat in the garage for another few minutes. When the door had lifted, she had been surprised to see Dillon's car parked on her customary right side. Callie was usually here much earlier than Dillon, who sometimes didn't come home until long after she went to bed.

Gathering her strength to go inside, she reached for the car door handle, then suddenly stopped. Dillon's words from lunch today came back to her as if she were hearing them for the first time. Dillon had said that *she* was the one who had to put on an act when they were in public. Did that mean Dillon didn't? The door leading into the house opened and the woman in question stood on the threshold.

"Is everything all right, Callie?" Dillon approached the car. "You've been sitting out here for a while. Do you need anything?" Dillon looked into the backseat and toward the trunk of the car. "Callie?" Dillon asked again, after Callie hadn't answered any of her questions.

Callie turned when she saw Dillon, who seemed to be an angel watching out for her—her guardian angel. Callie's heart jumped. Dillon's concern for her appeared to be real, but she had thought that Dillon married her because she loved her. Dillon hadn't destroyed only Callie's trust in her; she had destroyed her trust in herself. Callie's serious misjudgment had shaken her faith and self-confidence more than she ever expected.

"Everything's fine. Just thinking for a minute." Callie gathered her things and Dillon opened her door.

The garage was large but she had parked closer to the left wall than she usually did, and she had to squeeze by Dillon to get into the house. When she did, she inhaled the scent she had come to know as uniquely Dillon. The combination of musk and pine instantly took Callie back to being in Dillon's arms. She tripped on the step into the house.

Dillon reached out to catch her, her arm wrapping around Callie's waist. Their intimate contact sent a bolt of heat down Callie's spine, and it settled in her groin. When they touched as part of their public displays of matrimonial affection, Callie's body always reacted, but she had never revealed what their nearness actually did to her. But now her eyes were mere inches from Dillon's mouth and she fixed her gaze on lush red lips. Her breath quickened, and this time she didn't try to hide her response.

Callie looked from Dillon's lips to her eyes. She read the flame of desire in them that had become so familiar in their short time together. She could understand why Dillon had desired her. After all, she was an attractive woman. And she really didn't think Dillon had faked the dozens of times they had made love.

The seconds ticked by and neither one moved. Callie could no more forget the way her body responded and the thrill of Dillon's touch than she could forget her own name. She missed lying next to

Dillon in the quiet stillness just before dawn. The way their bodies talked to each other in the darkness of the night, conversing easily over a cup of coffee or fixing dinner together. No matter how hard she tried to deny the fact, she was still in love with Dillon Matthews. Dillon must have read something on her face because the color of her eyes darkened and she licked her lips.

Callie tried to remind herself that everything was different now. She had clearly stipulated that this marriage was in name only and Dillon would have to fulfill her lust somewhere else.

But that thought troubled Callie. How long would a woman like Dillon go without sex with her before she decided to venture out? Dillon was a sexy, sensual woman that other women found desirable, and she would have no trouble finding someone, or multiple someones, to ease her ache. She and Dillon hadn't promised to remain faithful during their chaste marriage, however long it might last. Suddenly the thought of Dillon touching another woman, or worse yet, another woman touching her, made Callie jealous.

Dillon's heart was racing and her pulse was pounding so hard she thought it must be echoing off the garage walls. Callie felt so good in her arms. When Callie stumbled, her body was stiff, as if she was anticipating a fall. Then she relaxed, molding into Dillon with a familiarity due to hours of lovemaking.

Dillon wanted to kiss her, needed to kiss her. She could practically taste the sweetness of the lips that were so near. Callie's lips moved even closer and she didn't know whether it was Callie or her that was moving, but she didn't care. In another second she would be kissing her. It wouldn't be a chaste, pretend kiss but a kiss fueled by passion and desire, and that was all that mattered.

At the first touch of their lips Callie thought she might faint. Dillon's kisses were exquisite, and sometimes she was able to come just from them alone. Dillon was tentative yet possessive. She nibbled at the edges of Callie's mouth, her tongue dancing on her lips as if waiting for her to invite her in. It didn't take long before she did. As Dillon's tongue filled her mouth, Callie turned and pressed her body completely against Dillon's unyielding form. Dillon's arms circled her waist and Callie wrapped her arms around

Dillon's neck, completely forgetting what she was doing or why she shouldn't be doing it.

It could have been hours or it could have been minutes before Callie lifted her head, gasping for breath. They were both panting heavily, and Callie enjoyed watching the quick rise and fall of Dillon's chest. Dillon's nipples hardened, and a tight fist of anticipation knotted the pit of Callie's stomach.

"I want you, Callie. I need you," Dillon said, barely able to speak because her passion almost choked her. She ached for Callie. Not just her touch, but because she longed so desperately to have her back again, in her life, with her. What she felt for Callie was more than lust. She loved her and wanted the good days and the bad, the joy and the sorrow, the passionate nights and the nights of simply holding each other while they slept. Her life was nothing without Callie.

The ringing of Callie's cell phone startled Dillon. The shrill sound continued for a few seconds before she even realized what it was. "Don't answer it," Dillon practically begged, but the moment was gone. The tension in Callie's body told her that as quickly as it was upon them it had passed, leaving a trail of white-hot embers. Reluctantly, Dillon released her. Callie stepped away at the same time, clutching the phone.

Chapter Twenty-one

"A re you nuts?" Greg looked at Dillon as if she had lost her mind.

"No, Greg, I'm not. I've already spoken to the mayor and it's a done deal. She plans to announce it this afternoon." Dillon shuffled some papers on her desk, finally locating what she was looking for.

"Dillon, the land alone is worth millions, not to mention how much money you would make once it's developed."

Greg wasn't telling her something she didn't already know. If anything, he was underestimating the value of the parcel of land near the central corridor of town.

The scene in the garage with Callie a week ago haunted Dillon, and they had gingerly sidestepped each other ever since. Callie seemed afraid to be alone with her for too long. Dillon herself struggled to keep her emotions in check and more times than not spent the night lying awake in her bed.

Driving to work the morning after the garage incident, she crystallized the thoughts that had been bouncing around in her head. What good was all of her wealth if she didn't have Callie to share it with? She didn't need another skyscraper with her name on the cornerstone, or another shopping center on her résumé. Her skills and talent had gotten her everything she ever dreamed of, and greed had cost her the only thing that mattered. She couldn't change the past, but she could change her behavior going forward.

"Greg, it's a done deal," she replied, effectively shutting off any further conversation. Dillon wouldn't change her mind. If anything, this was only the beginning.

❖

"Callie, turn on the TV. Channel 15, hurry, you'll miss it."

"Good grief, Audrey, what's going on?" Callie asked, searching for the remote. After finding it under the pillow on the couch, she hit the power button. The face of Mayor Roberta James in front of a microphone materialized an instant before the sound hit her ears.

"And I'm pleased to announce that Dillon Matthews has donated the land that the city so desperately needs for the new public library." The mayor was practically beaming. Behind her was the drawing of the library that had been featured in the paper a few weeks ago. "As you know, for the past few years we have been searching for the right property at a price the taxpayers could afford, and we had been unsuccessful until Dillon Matthews called my office last week."

Callie sat on the couch and turned up the volume. She couldn't hear the questions from the reporter, but the mayor's voice was clear as she patiently answered each one.

"No, there are no strings attached other than the land must be used for the library and a small park. I can't speak to Ms. Matthews's motives other than to say that this donation is very generous. She specifically told me that she did not want to be here this afternoon because this is not about her. It's about the city getting what it very much needs. No, we had not been in negotiations with Ms. Matthews prior to this. This parcel of land was far too expensive for the city budget. The county has appraised it at eight point five million dollars."

Callie didn't hear any more answers, Audrey's voice coming from the phone receiver reminding her that she was still clutching it. "I'm sorry, what did you say?"

"I asked if you knew she was going to do this." Audrey was a reporter for the local newspaper and hated being scooped.

"No, I didn't." Callie didn't add that Dillon no longer discussed her business with her. Callie was glad Audrey couldn't see her humiliation at not knowing what Dillon had done.

"Wow, what a tax write-off. Eight point five million dollars. And she just *gave* it to them?"

Callie was still processing the information. She knew how much every piece of property meant to Dillon, and if this report was true, she was stunned. Especially if she gave it with no strings. She had expected Dillon to insist on having her name on the building, at least.

❖

"The mayor has invited us to a reception she's throwing for the dedication of the new art museum."

Dillon's statement puzzled Callie. It was after ten and Dillon had come home from the office at this same time for the past few days. She had hardly said more than three things to her since their kiss a week ago. Callie had to find out about a huge land deal on the news and now Dillon expected her to be elbow candy for some politico? Callie didn't know whether to be hurt or insulted. She wanted to choose the latter, but she really wasn't in charge of her emotions anymore.

"I'll bet she does." Callie hoped she sounded as sarcastic as she felt.

"I take it you know about the library land?"

"Yes, and I had to find out when Audrey called me and told me to turn on the TV. Do you know how that made me feel, I mean how that made me look?" She quickly corrected herself. She was hurt that Dillon hadn't shared the news with her, but she didn't want her to know that fact. "I'm your wife, Dillon, I should have known."

Dillon understood why Callie was so upset. Even though it was Callie's idea to be her wife in name only, anyone else's spouse would have known. She hadn't thought of that point. Her plan to show Callie that she meant more to her than a piece of land had backfired.

"You're right, I should have told you. I'm sorry. I didn't intend to embarrass you."

"What did you intend?"

Dillon debated whether to tell Callie. She probably wouldn't believe her even if she did. It was too soon. "Call it a moment of civic duty."

Callie looked at her as if trying to detect any trace of deceit, but she wouldn't find any.

❖

Callie learned of several more "moments of civic duty" over the next few weeks. Dillon had left the contents of her briefcase strewn across the couch one evening, and when Callie bent to pick up several papers that had fallen onto the floor, she couldn't help but glance at the top sheet. She recognized the logo of the snack shop next to the florist shop and skimmed the contents. The owner was thanking Dillon for renegotiating their contract and reducing their rent substantially. *Reducing their rent?* Callie laid the papers on the table, not sure if she should feel guilty for snooping or glad she did.

One afternoon Dillon called the florist shop and told her that she had just sold a parcel of land at a reduced rate to a large philanthropic organization that provided affordable housing to low-income families. She said that she wanted Callie to know because the group would be issuing a press release the next day.

The phone was ringing when Callie stepped inside the house, balancing a bag of groceries in one arm and her gym bag in the other.

"Hello?"

"Callie, it's Bill," the familiar voice said.

She dropped her bag on the floor and set the groceries on the counter. Wedging the phone between her ear and shoulder, she used both hands to unpack the perishables. "Bill, hello. How are you? How's Phyllis?"

"I'm fine, Phyl is fine. How are you? Is this a good time?"

Callie put the ice cream in the freezer and the milk, eggs, and cottage cheese in the refrigerator. "It is now. What's up?"

"Is Dillon there? Oh, my, that was rude. Sorry. As much as I'd love to chat with you, I called to talk to your mysterious wife."

"Mysterious?" Callie was intrigued by the description.

"Yes, it's a mystery as to why she hasn't signed the final escrow paper. Without it, the sale can't close. As hot as she was for that piece of land, I would have expected her to move heaven and earth to close escrow. It's just been sitting there ready for the past few weeks. The property isn't officially hers until escrow closes. I'm just checking to see if there's a problem. I understand the parcel-number problem has been resolved, so she just needs to sign the revised filing."

Dillon had put a hold on the closing? Callie suddenly realized she hadn't heard anything more about Gateway for several months. Dillon had been hot to get moving on the project, and she made a mental note to ask her about it when she got home.

"I'm sorry, Bill, I haven't a clue, and she had to go out of town for a few days." Callie left out the part that she didn't know exactly when Dillon would be home. Dillon had called earlier in the day but told her only that there was a problem with the zoning commission in St. Louis and she was on her way to the airport. "I'll tell her you called when I talk to her."

"Thanks, I appreciate it. Sorry, Callie, but I've gotta run. I'm meeting Phyllis for dinner in twenty minutes. I just thought I'd try to catch Dillon at home."

"Tell Phyllis we said hello and have her call me. It's our turn to host, maybe next weekend?"

"Sounds good. I'll give Phyl your message."

Callie set the receiver back into the charger but didn't let go. She stood that way for several minutes pondering Bill's call. She hadn't signed the final papers? What was the problem? What did that mean?

Her questions went unanswered for the remainder of the evening, and it wasn't until after nine when she realized stupidly that she had been waiting to hear the sound of the garage door opening.

Her heart raced as it did lately every time she was about to see Dillon. It didn't matter if she was coming home from the office or walking into the kitchen in the middle of the weekend. More than a pitter-patter was going on in her chest. Callie was feeling the same way about Dillon as she did before her deception was exposed. She anxiously waited for Dillon every night. Hoped that it was her every time the phone rang. Wondered what she was doing in her room down the hall.

CHAPTER TWENTY-TWO

"Don't do this, Callie."

"Michael, I know what I'm doing."

"So do I, and I'm telling you to stop. How long have you known?"

Callie sighed, suddenly very tired. She had come to see Michael for her weekly visit and one thing led to another, and before she knew it she had told him everything. He was furious at Dillon for her deception and more so at Callie for going along with it. "It doesn't matter."

"Yes, it does."

The guard stared at Michael, who had raised his voice.

"No, it doesn't, Michael. What matters is that your new trial starts next week. You need to stay focused on getting out of here. I'm fine, and this is nothing if it gets you out."

Her brother looked better than he had the last time she had come to visit him, but his face still showed signs of anxiety. He had told her not to get her hopes up on the outcome of his new trial, but Callie couldn't be anything but optimistic.

"I spoke to Dillon a while back." Callie raised her head instantly at the mention of Dillon's name. "I called her. I wanted to thank her for everything she was doing for me."

"What did she say?" Dillon hadn't told Callie about Michael's call.

"That she loves you."

Michael's words cut through Callie. "What?"

"That she loves you. I told her that you were in love with her and I didn't want to see you get hurt."

"You told her what?"

This time the guard looked at her.

"Cal, I see a lot of things in here. I've gotten pretty good at reading a situation, and when you two are together, the way your face lights up when you talk about her, it's as plain as the nose on my face. I don't condone what she did and I don't like what you're doing, but in a lot of ways I understand. People will do almost anything when they want something bad enough. Look at you. Isn't that what you're doing?"

Callie didn't respond, still trying to gather her thoughts from the whiplash turn of events. One minute her brother was furious at her, the next telling her what Dillon had done was okay.

His voice continued through the static of the receiver. "You might not be ready to admit it, but you had better open your eyes or the best thing that ever happened to you is going to walk out of your life."

❖

The slamming door behind Callie made her jump. She hadn't slept much in the past week, her nerves on end waiting for Michael's trial. His attorney, Raymond Nixon, was optimistic and had told her to remain calm when it was her turn on the stand, and today was the day. Because she was a witness, she had not been allowed in the courtroom prior to her testimony. She looked to the left, where her brother sat next to Nixon. He wore a dark suit that Callie had picked out for him, along with a crisp white shirt and blue striped tie that Dillon contributed. His hair was recently cut and his shoes shined. He smiled reassuringly as she walked up the aisle toward the witness chair. Dillon was sitting directly behind Michael, with Audrey to her left and Ross on her right. Bill and Phyllis were in the row behind them. Without a doubt, this was her family now and Callie felt their love and support. Her nerves settled.

Her hand was steady as she was sworn in, and after stating

her name and address she focused her attention on Nixon. His questions were clear and Callie's voice grew stronger as she told what happened that night four years ago. She looked each juror in the eye as she recounted the chain of events. She focused on the women when she spoke about the attempted rape and saw several of them wince when she described how one of her attackers tied her hands to the bed while the other held her legs as he fumbled with the zipper on his pants.

The prosecuting attorney took his turn and aggressively peppered Callie with questions. She remained calm and answered his questions truthfully and confidently. Her testimony this time was far different than at Michael's first trial. Gone was her naiveté in thinking that all she had to do was tell what happened and the jury would find him not guilty. She was much wiser this time in how she answered the questions.

She didn't look at Dillon during her entire testimony. Reliving the incident while knowing that her brother's life was at stake was stressful enough. She didn't need the added turmoil of Dillon's reaction to distract her.

They had talked about the trial for the past several evenings, Dillon coming home before six every night. She now knew the whole story and had reacted the way Callie had expected. She was incensed at what the attackers had done to her, and even more exasperated over Michael's conviction. It was almost as if she wanted to march down to the court and knock some sense into the judge who had presided over Michael's trial. Dillon's apparent care for her brother touched Callie, and the cold edge around her heart began to thaw.

Dismissed from the stand, Callie walked out of the courtroom as confident as when she walked in.

❖

"The jury's back." Raymond Nixon's voice practically boomed through the phone line. "You've got thirty minutes to get here."

Callie dropped the flowers she was arranging, grabbed her keys, and ran out the door. When she reached the courtroom, it was practically empty. She sat on the hard bench behind Michael with the family of the man he'd killed on the other side. It struck her that the seating arrangements were nearly identical to those at a wedding. The family of the defendant on one side, the victim on the other.

A movement out of the corner of her eye caught her attention. Dillon was sliding into the row wearing a hurried look and a warm smile.

"Ross called," Dillon said to her unasked question. "He said you took off out of the shop like a bat out of hell, and it could only be one thing. I'll leave if you don't want me here. I got here as soon as I could. I'm glad I was in time." During the four days the jury had deliberated, Dillon had not asked if she wanted her to be there when the verdict was read, but obviously Dillon wanted to be here for her.

"Thank you." Callie took Dillon's hand. It was warm and strong, and she hung on to it like it was a lifeline.

Callie jumped when the judge banged his gavel. Dillon covered her hand with her free one and scooted closer. The preliminaries over, Callie held her breath when the judge asked Michael to rise as the jury read their verdict.

❖

Dillon heard a sound behind her, and when she turned around, her world stopped. Callie stood in the doorway of the living room sheathed in a black dress that was almost like a second skin. The neckline plunged, revealing more than a hint of cleavage where Dillon had paused so long ago and nibbled on her way from Callie's smooth neck to parts farther south. The bodice of the dress supported her full breasts and fell straight to the hem. The entire dress was held up by two straps so thin Dillon was afraid they would break under the weight of the dress. Sheer black nylons covered her legs.

Dillon heard nothing but the banging of her heart against her chest, her breath rattling through tight lungs beneath her starched shirt. Her mind went blank and she stood there unable to move. Callie was absolutely beautiful.

They were dressed for the art museum opening Dillon had mentioned a few weeks ago. Dillon hadn't wanted to go but Callie had insisted. She wanted to celebrate. Michael had been found not guilty and was due to be released as soon as the paperwork was processed.

Callie barely remembered what happened in the courtroom when the verdict was read. All she recalled were the two words that she would never forget. Dillon told her that she had practically fainted with relief and then jumped up and hugged Michael, tears streaming down both their faces. Dillon thanked Nixon and shook his hand before the attorney grabbed his briefcase, muttered something to Michael, and walked out of the courtroom. It was only later that afternoon that Callie calmed down enough to remember the museum opening was that night.

She felt fabulous, and the look in Dillon's eyes made her feel desired. Dillon was not even trying to mask how much she wanted her, her eyes raking over her body several times. Callie noticed a faint blush to Dillon's neck just above her collar, and her chest moved in shallow breaths. If she didn't know Dillon, she would be frightened by the look of hunger in her eyes. As it was, her own heart was pounding, and the pulse point between her legs was beating the strongest.

Dillon didn't know how long she stood there gaping at Callie like a schoolboy, but she finally found her voice. "You look wonderful."

She had no idea how she would possibly get through the evening with Callie looking like that and her feeling like this. She ached for Callie. Her fingers tingled as she relived the feel of Callie's soft skin, her palms cupping the weight of her breasts. She wanted to gather Callie in her arms and simply kiss her until the sun came up.

Dillon took a step forward and stopped when she realized that was exactly what she was about to do. But she couldn't. She wouldn't. She had made an agreement with Callie, and she would prove she was true to her word.

But as of this morning, their agreement was no longer valid. Michael would be released and Callie would leave. As much as

Dillon wanted her, needed her, yearned for her, she had to wait for Callie to come to her. It would be the only way she could really have her.

Callie was surprised when Dillon stopped a few steps in front of her. Dillon had been nearing her and Callie's pulse had increased in anticipation. Now a pang of disappointment rang through her when Dillon stopped. She'd felt alive in Dillon's arms, and she wanted to feel that way again. But she didn't have the nerve to swallow her pride and step into them.

"Thank you. You look very nice yourself," Callie finally replied. Dillon had chosen a plum-colored silk suit that was so dark it could pass for black. The white tuxedo shirt was unbuttoned at the collar, exposed the pulsing vein in her neck. Callie held her breath. Her senses, already on high alert just from being near Dillon, were now on overload. Dillon's breath caressed her ear.

"Thanks. Personally I think it's just an excuse for everybody to get dressed up and try to impress each other with their fancy clothes and jewels." Dillon thought she felt herself smile, or at least produce the hint of a smile. "And speaking of jewels, don't go away."

Dillon hurried into the other room and returned carrying a dark blue box. Stepping behind Callie, she lifted the sapphire necklace she had bought in Montreal from its silk bed and caught her and Callie's reflection in the mirror hanging on the wall. Their eyes locked as she placed the vibrant stone against Callie's smooth neck. The familiar scent of Callie's perfume hung in the air around them and Dillon drank it in. Her hands were shaking so badly she couldn't get the delicate clasp closed and had to drag her eyes away from Callie's to secure the two ends. Her heart was beating hard in her chest when she returned her gaze to the mirror.

Callie was looking at her the way she had when they stood side by side at the altar. It seemed like a lifetime ago. Dillon's breathing matched the shallow rise and fall of Callie's chest, which was accentuated by the glimmering gemstone. Their eyes held and she couldn't speak for a minute.

"You look beautiful." It was a simple statement, but filled with honest sentiment.

"Dillon, it's lovely," Callie replied, her fingers caressing the chain. "You shouldn't have."

Callie's voice was breathy and chills scampered up and down Dillon's spine. "I saw it and immediately thought of you. I knew it would look stunning on you." Dillon's hands rested on Callie's shoulders where they had landed after she closed the clasp. Unable to fight the urge to caress the bare skin under her fingertips, she let her hands drop and stepped back, trying to regain control of her emotions.

In control. That was an interesting concept these days. The only thing in control was Callie's grip on her heart. Her body couldn't forget their kiss in the garage, and Dillon didn't know if she could physically handle another situation with the same ending.

The reception was well under way when they arrived. A red carpet led the way to the front door, and camera flashes popped as Dillon led Callie toward the ornate doors. Callie's hand was in the crook of her arm, and Dillon stopped just before they stepped inside. She leaned down, her lips close to Callie's ear.

"Ready?" When Callie nodded, Dillon moved even closer, indulging herself for just a moment in Callie's fresh, clean scent. She moved her head back enough to gaze into Callie's eyes. "You are going to be the most beautiful woman in the room." Callie's eyes sparkled, and what Dillon saw deep in her eyes made her add, "Don't forget, I love you and you have to pretend that you love me." Dillon ended her sentence by placing a tender, lingering kiss on Callie's lips.

Callie practically jumped out of her skin when Dillon kissed her. Instinctively her free hand found its way to the back of Dillon's neck. Dillon started to withdraw, and Callie held Dillon's lips against hers for a moment longer. When she finally released her, they were both breathing heavily. A flood of emotions tore through Callie. She was confused. She should be appalled by Dillon's kiss, by the mere fact that she had to be near her, let alone allow her to fawn all over her and kiss her whenever she pleased. But she wasn't. Callie couldn't get close enough to Dillon. Couldn't have enough of her kisses. She was ashamed at her reaction to someone who had treated her as badly and with as much disrespect as Dillon had. But she wasn't too ashamed to not want to be intimate with her again.

Dillon straightened with a hint of her former confidence and hesitated, as if waiting for Callie to say something. But when she didn't, Dillon said, "Shall we?" They stepped inside.

Callie clung to Dillon's arm not out of fear but for strength. Dillon's kiss had made her legs weak, and the tenderness in her eyes made her dizzy. If Dillon wanted she could take her right here, right now in front of everybody, and Callie would let her. She was out of control and somehow had to pull it together before she made a fool of herself.

Dillon led her to the bar, stopping to talk to several dignitaries and museum patrons along the way. Callie saw very few familiar faces, and she detected something different in Dillon's voice when she introduced her as her wife. Dillon had called Callie her wife many times before and after she discovered Dillon's ruse, but tonight she said it with a lilt and inflection that had never been there before. Dillon's rhythmic words warmed the blood in her veins every time she heard them.

"Dance with me?"

Dillon's question was phrased in such a way that it sounded more like a plea than a request. Callie knew she was fighting with fire, but she could no more refuse Dillon this request than she could stop thinking about her.

They glided onto the dance floor and Callie slid easily into Dillon's embrace. Dillon's hands shook and Callie had to force herself to concentrate on the steps of the dance when all she really wanted to do was stand perfectly still and memorize the feel of Dillon's arms around her. The dance floor was suddenly crowded and Callie silently thanked God for her intervention. It was perfectly acceptable for Dillon to slow her steps to practically nothing in order to mesh with the other dancers doing the same.

Dillon whispered for Callie to relax. But how in the hell was she supposed to relax when her heart was racing like a thoroughbred? She wanted every inch of Dillon's body against hers. She was both afraid and hopeful that Dillon would slide her strong leg between hers. Dillon's hands traveled up and down Callie's back, stopping just shy of inappropriateness for such a gathering. Nobody seemed to mind that two women were dancing together, and when the song ended she stepped out of Dillon's arms.

"I need something to drink. Preferably something short and cold." Callie snickered at her own words. She had held something tall and hot in her hands just a minute ago, and she had let go. *Make up your mind, girl.*

"Care to share?" Dillon asked, grinning.

Callie stumbled for a witty reply but came up empty. "Not really, no. I don't think you'd find it nearly as amusing as I do."

Dillon took Callie's hand and nabbed a passing waiter, snagging two glasses of champagne. "Try me. You might be surprised."

Callie suddenly looked at Dillon and felt as if she were seeing her for the first time. Something Dillon had said earlier rushed back to her, something about how Callie was the one who had to pretend they were in love. She had pondered the statement once, but it hadn't totally clicked then. It did now, though, and the realization was as loud as the ticking of a grandfather clock. Did that mean Dillon didn't have to pretend?

Speculation danced in her head. What if Dillon did love her? What if sometime during this three-act play Dillon had fallen in love with her? What would she do and, most importantly, how would she know? Could she trust Dillon? Could she trust herself? She had already proved herself inept in that department. The thought terrified her.

Callie took her drink from Dillon and their fingers touched slightly. She stared at Dillon and met dark pools already gazing at her. Callie's knees threatened to buckle when Dillon looked away.

"Here comes Phil Privett, the president of the Tillman Club. He's been trying to trap me into becoming a member for years. Oh, man, who's that child hanging all over him? It certainly is not his wife."

Callie watched Dillon make nice to Privett and his squeeze, who Callie guessed was barely legal, let alone old enough for the beer in her hand. As Dillon feared, he tried several different ways to pin her down to join the group he referred to as the "movers and shakers of the community." Dillon expertly evaded his every attempt, and he finally took his girlfriend and left.

Many other people clamored for Dillon's attention, and Callie had very little time alone with her for the rest of the evening. She was disappointed because now that she suspected Dillon felt more for her than she admitted, Callie wanted to study her. She wanted to dissect Dillon's facial expressions when she talked to her, to determine whether her hands trembled or her muscles tensed when Callie touched her. All of these subtle signs would tell her if Dillon was really in love. But Callie needed to pay attention to the conversation and Dillon at the same time. She found the first a bore and the second a challenge.

"You haven't mentioned anything about Gateway in a while. Why not?"

"I haven't?" Dillon asked, feigning confusion.

"You know you haven't."

Callie had passed on Bill's message, but Dillon had hemmed and hawed, trying to put Callie off by claiming she would look into the escrow situation. She had never said anything else about it because she wanted to forget that shameful part of her past.

"No. I haven't."

"Don't you want the deal to close?"

Dillon didn't answer. Instead she glanced around the room looking for an escape.

"Don't you?"

Dillon frowned at Callie's persistence. She wondered why it was so important to her. It was one of the threads that held them together, and as soon as she signed the papers the county clerk would stamp them as filed and the thin strand would break. That was another reason she hadn't.

"No. I guess it's not as important as I once thought it was."

Dillon looked at Callie standing beside her. She had been in this position all evening, and it felt good. She was proud of the way Callie had conducted herself at the trial and at the public functions where she accompanied Dillon. She was overcome with a sense of sadness at the knowledge it would all soon end.

Before another person could come up to her, Dillon swept Callie back onto the dance floor and changed the subject. "Sorry about all the attention. I don't get out much to these kinds of things and now I know why." She quirked her mouth.

"You seem to be the belle of the ball," Callie replied, melting into Dillon's arms.

Dillon chuckled. "Hardly. They just use me as an excuse to get closer to you. I said you would be the most beautiful woman here, and you are." Dillon wished there was another way to convince Callie just how lovely she was.

"I think not."

Dillon leaned back enough to see Callie's face. Their lower bodies were still touching, and the arching of her back pressed them even closer. "You need to get out more, my dear. Every man in the room has had his eye on you at one time or another this evening."

"And you've been strutting around like a peacock because of it," Callie teased.

"I didn't think you noticed." Dillon waited a second or two to let her comment sink in. "Do you blame me? With you as my wife, everybody wants to be me. That's a heady, powerful feeling."

Callie playfully slapped Dillon's arm. "Don't let it go to your head, Ms. Matthews."

Dillon laughed, enjoying their light banter. They hadn't talked like this in ages. She was relaxed and felt like they were gliding across the dance floor. "I'm sure you'll keep me in line, Mrs. Matthews. After all, isn't that what wives are for?"

"Is that what you want your wife to do? Keep you in line?"

"No," Dillon answered simply and seriously.

"What do you want?" Callie asked, not sure if she was ready for the answer. Dillon looked at her as if trying to decide if her question was serious or not. She seemed to make a decision.

"I want a woman who loves me. Not my money, or my reputation, or the things I can give her. Someone who wants to build a life with me. I want a woman who will stand behind me when I need support, in front of me when I don't know where I'm going, and beside me all the time. I want her to hold my head when I'm sick and kick my butt when I need it. I want her to be crazy about me when I deserve it, and angry at me and able to forgive me when I do something stupid."

The music played in the background, but Callie didn't hear anything but the words flowing from Dillon's lips. She had never heard anything so simple yet poetic. That was exactly what she wanted in a partner as well, and what she wanted to be to someone. Dillon amazed her. She had far deeper emotions than people gave her credit for. More and more, Callie had discovered these sensitive little pieces of Dillon, and she liked what she saw.

"Anybody meet those requirements?"

Dillon inhaled sharply. "Not recently."

Callie's stomach jumped into her throat. *Could it be?* "Then someone earlier?"

"Definitely."

"Anyone I know?" Callie was stepping out on a very shaky limb. She was risking everything if she had misjudged Dillon again, but the entire nightmare with Michael had taught her one very important thing—to live every day as if it were her last. She would never again pass up the opportunity to tell someone she loved them.

"I'm not sure. She has definitely changed in the time I've known her."

"How so?" Callie wanted to know what Dillon thought of her.

"Well, let's see." Dillon stopped and looked deep into her eyes. "She is much stronger than she was when we first met." She ran her fingers through Callie's hair, the strands falling through her fingers. "Her hair is a little longer." She caressed Callie's cheek with the back of her trembling fingers. "Her eyes sparkle more, especially today. And she is more beautiful now than when I first saw her sitting on a bar stool nursing a light beer."

Dillon lowered her head and tentatively kissed her. Callie wrapped her arms around Dillon's neck and pulled her closer, aware that the predominantly straight crowd must be staring, but not caring.

Her body swayed, and she wasn't sure if she was responding to the music or molding herself into Dillon's hard, hot form. Dillon's kiss was soft and Callie could tell she was holding back her passion. But Callie didn't want her to. She was tired of holding in her feelings for Dillon, and she wanted to possess every inch and to feel every molecule of her.

Dillon pulled away, breathing heavily. She had gambled by letting Callie know how she felt about her. She had been afraid Callie would laugh in her face and call her a fool, but she would be a bigger fool if she let her walk away.

Now she was certain nobody would ever exist for her except for Callie, who filled her arms to overflowing. She wanted her now, tomorrow, and forever. She rolled the dice again. "Will you marry me?"

Callie's heart raced faster than it had the first time Dillon asked her. This time she was certain Dillon meant it the way it was supposed to be. Dillon loved her and wanted her. Not some piece of land, not as a means to another accomplishment, but simply her.

"On one condition."

"Anything."

"Sign the papers."

About the Author

Julie Cannon is a native of Phoenix, Arizona, where she lives with her partner Laura and their two children. Julie's day job is in Corporate America and her nights are spent bringing to life the stories that bounce around in her head throughout the day. When Julie's not writing, she and Laura spend their time camping and lounging around the pool with their kids.

Julie is the author of four romances published by Bold Strokes Books—*Come and Get Me, Heart 2 Heart, Heartland, Uncharted Passage*—and is hard at work on her next novel, *Power Play*. She has short story selections in *Erotic Interludes 4: Extreme Passions, Erotic Interludes 5: Road Games*, and *Romantic Interludes 1: Discovery*. Visit Julie at www.juliecannon.com.

Books Available From Bold Strokes Books

The Sublime and Spirited Voyage of *Original Sin* by Colette Moody. Pirate Gayle Malvern finds the presence of an abducted seamstress, Celia Pierce, a welcome distraction until the captive comes to mean more to her than is wise. (978-1-60282-054-8)

Suspect Passions by VK Powell. Can two women, a city attorney and a beat cop, put aside their differences long enough to see that they're perfect for each other? (978-1-60282-053-1)

Just Business by Julie Cannon. Two women who come together—each for her own selfish needs—discover that love can never be as simple as a business transaction. (978-1-60282-052-4)

Sistine Heresy by Justine Saracen. Adrianna Borgia, survivor of the Borgia court, presents Michelangelo with the greatest temptations of his life while struggling with soul-threatening desires for the painter Raphaela. (978-1-60282-051-7)

Radical Encounters by Radclyffe. An out-of-bounds, outside-the-lines collection of provocative, superheated erotica by award-winning romance and erotica author Radclyffe. (978-1-60282-050-0)

Thief of Always by Kim Baldwin & Xenia Alexiou. Stealing a diamond to save the world should be easy for Elite Operative Mishael Taylor, but she didn't figure on love getting in the way. (978-1-60282-049-4)

X by JD Glass. When X-hacker Charlie Riven is framed for a crime she didn't commit, she accepts help from an unlikely source—sexy Treasury Agent Elaine Harper. (978-1-60282-048-7)

The Middle of Somewhere by Clifford Henderson. Eadie T. Pratt sets out on a road trip in search of a new life and ends up in the middle of somewhere she never expected. (978-1-60282-047-0)

Paybacks by Gabrielle Goldsby. Cameron Howard wants to avoid her old nemesis Mackenzie Brandt but their high school reunion brings up more than just memories. (978-1-60282-046-3)

Uncross My Heart by Andrews & Austin. When a radio talk show diva sets out to interview a female priest, the two women end up at odds, and neither heaven nor earth is safe from their feelings. (978-1-60282-045-6)

Fireside by Cate Culpepper. Mac, a therapist, and Abby, a nurse, fall in love against the backdrop of friendship, healing, and defending one's own within the Fireside shelter. (978-1-60282-044-9)

Green Eyed Monster by Gill McKnight. Mickey Rapowski believes her former boss has cheated her out of a small fortune, so she kidnaps the girlfriend and demands compensation—just a straightforward abduction that goes so wrong when Mickey falls for her captive. (978-1-60282-042-5)

Blind Faith by Diane and Jacob Anderson-Minshall. When private investigator Yoshi Yakamota and the Blind Eye Detective Agency are hired to find a woman's missing sister, the assignment seems fairly mundane—but in the detective business, the ordinary can quickly become deadly. (978-1-60282-041-8)

A Pirate's Heart by Catherine Friend. When rare book librarian Emma Boyd searches for a long-lost treasure map, she learns the hard way that pirates still exist in today's world—some modern pirates steal maps, others steal hearts. (978-1-60282-040-1)

Trails Merge by Rachel Spangler. Parker Riley escapes the high-powered world of politics to Campbell Carson's ski resort—and their mutual attraction produces anything but smooth running. (978-1-60282-039-5)

Dreams of Bali by C.J. Harte. Madison Barnes worships work, power, and success, and she's never allowed anyone to interfere—that is, until she runs into Karlie Henderson Stockard. Aeros EBook (978-1-60282-070-8)

The Limits of Justice by John Morgan Wilson. Benjamin Justice and reporter Alexandra Templeton search for a killer in a mysterious compound in the remote California desert. (978-1-60282-060-9)

Designed for Love by Erin Dutton. Jillian Sealy and Wil Johnson don't much like each other, but they do have to work together—and what they desire most is not what either of them had planned. (978-1-60282-038-8)

Calling the Dead by Ali Vali. Six months after Hurricane Katrina, NOLA Detective Sept Savoie is a cop who thinks making a relationship work is harder than catching a serial killer—but her current case may prove her wrong. (978-1-60282-037-1)

Shots Fired by MJ Williamz. Kyla and Echo seem to have the perfect relationship and the perfect life until someone shoots at Kyla—and Echo is the most likely suspect. (978-1-60282-035-7)

truelesbianlove.com by Carsen Taite. Mackenzie Lewis and Dr. Jordan Wagner have very different ideas about love, but they discover that truelesbianlove is closer than a click away. Aeros EBook (978-1-60282-069-2)

Justice at Risk by John Morgan Wilson. Benjamin Justice's blind date leads to a rare opportunity for legitimate work, but a reckless risk changes his life forever. (978-1-60282-059-3)

Run to Me by Lisa Girolami. Burned by the four-letter word called love, the only thing Beth Standish wants to do is run for—or maybe from—her life. (978-1-60282-034-0)

Split the Aces by Jove Belle. In the neon glare of Sin City, two women ride a wave of passion that threatens to consume them in a world of fast money and fast times. (978-1-60282-033-3)

Uncharted Passage by Julie Cannon. Two women on a vacation that turns deadly face down one of nature's most ruthless killers—and find themselves falling in love. (978-1-60282-032-6)

Night Call by Radclyffe. All medevac helicopter pilot Jett McNally wants to do is fly and forget about the horror and heartbreak she left behind in the Middle East, but anesthesiologist Tristan Holmes has other plans. (978-1-60282-031-9)

Lake Effect Snow by C.P. Rowlands. News correspondent Annie T. Booker and FBI Agent Sarah Moore struggle to stay one step ahead of disaster as Annie's life becomes the war zone she once reported on. Aeros EBook (978-1-60282-068-5)

Revision of Justice by John Morgan Wilson. Murder shifts into high gear, propelling Benjamin Justice into a raging fire that consumes the Hollywood Hills, burning steadily toward the famous Hollywood Sign—and the identity of a cold-blooded killer. (978-1-60282-058-6)

I Dare You by Larkin Rose. Stripper by night, corporate raider by day, Kelsey's only looking for sex and power, until she meets a woman who stirs her heart and her body. (978-1-60282-030-2)

Truth Behind the Mask by Lesley Davis. Erith Baylor is drawn to Sentinel Pagan Osborne's quiet strength, but the secrets between them strain duty and family ties. (978-1-60282-029-6)

Cooper's Deale by KI Thompson. Two would-be lovers and a decidedly inopportune murder spell trouble for Addy Cooper, no matter which way the cards fall. (978-1-60282-028-9)

Romantic Interludes 1: Discovery ed. by Radclyffe and Stacia Seaman. An anthology of sensual, erotic contemporary love stories from the best-selling Bold Strokes authors. (978-1-60282-027-2)

A Guarded Heart by Jennifer Fulton. The last place FBI Special Agent Pat Roussel expects to find herself is assigned to an illicit private security gig baby-sitting a celebrity. Aeros Ebook (978-1-60282-067-8)

Saving Grace by Jennifer Fulton. Champion swimmer Dawn Beaumont, injured in a car crash she caused, flees to Moon Island, where scientist Grace Ramsay welcomes her. Aeros Ebook (978-1-60282-066-1)

The Sacred Shore by Jennifer Fulton. Successful tech industry survivor Merris Randall does not believe in love at first sight until she meets Olivia Pearce. Aeros Ebook (978-1-60282-065-4)

Passion Bay by Jennifer Fulton. Two women from different ends of the earth meet in paradise. Author's expanded edition. Aeros Ebook (978-1-60282-064-7)

Never Wake by Gabrielle Goldsby. After a brutal attack, Emma Webster becomes a self-sentenced prisoner inside her condo—until the world outside her window goes silent. Aeros Ebook (978-1-60282-063-0)

The Caretaker's Daughter by Gabrielle Goldsby. Against the backdrop of a nineteenth-century English country estate, two women struggle to find love. Aeros Ebook (978-1-60282-062-3)

Simple Justice by John Morgan Wilson. When a pretty-boy cokehead is murdered, former LA reporter Benjamin Justice and his reluctant new partner, Alexandra Templeton, must unveil the real killer. (978-1-60282-057-9)

Remember Tomorrow by Gabrielle Goldsby. Cees Bannigan and Arieanna Simon find that a successful relationship rests in remembering the mistakes of the past. (978-1-60282-026-5)

Put Away Wet by Susan Smith. Jocelyn "Joey" Fellows has just been savagely dumped—when she posts an online personal ad, she discovers more than just the great sex she expected. (978-1-60282-025-8)

Homecoming by Nell Stark. Sarah Storm loses everything that matters— family, future dreams, and love—will her new "straight" roommate cause Sarah to take a chance at happiness? (978-1-60282-024-1)

The Three by Meghan O'Brien. A daring, provocative exploration of love and sexuality. Two lovers, Elin and Kael, struggle to survive in a postapocalyptic world. Aeros Ebook (978-1-60282-056-2)

Falling Star by Gill McKnight. Solley Rayner hopes a few weeks with her family will help heal her shattered dreams, but she hasn't counted on meeting a woman who stirs her heart. (978-1-60282-023-4)

Lethal Affairs by Kim Baldwin and Xenia Alexiou. Elite operative Domino is no stranger to peril, but her investigation of journalist Hayley Ward will test more than her skills. (978-1-60282-022-7)

A Place to Rest by Erin Dutton. Sawyer Drake doesn't know what she wants from life until she meets Jori Diamantina—only trouble is, Jori doesn't seem to share her desire. (978-1-60282-021-0)

Warrior's Valor by Gun Brooke. Dwyn Izsontro and Emeron D'Artansis must put aside personal animosity and unwelcome attraction to defeat an enemy of the Protector of the Realm. (978-1-60282-020-3)

Finding Home by Georgia Beers. Take two polar-opposite women with an attraction for one another they're trying desperately to ignore, throw in a far-too-observant dog, and then sit back and enjoy the romance. (978-1-60282-019-7)

Word of Honor by Radclyffe. All Secret Service Agent Cameron Roberts and First Daughter Blair Powell want is a small intimate wedding, but the paparazzi and a domestic terrorist have other plans. (978-1-60282-018-0)

Hotel Liaison by JLee Meyer. Two women searching through a secret past discover that their brief hotel liaison is only the beginning. Will they risk their careers—and their hearts—to follow through on their desires? (978-1-60282-017-3)

Love on Location by Lisa Girolami. Hollywood film producer Kate Nyland and artist Dawn Brock discover that love doesn't always follow the script. (978-1-60282-016-6)

Edge of Darkness by Jove Belle. Investigator Diana Collins charges at life with an irreverent comment and a right hook, but even those may not protect her heart from a charming villain. (978-1-60282-015-9)

Thirteen Hours by Meghan O'Brien. Workaholic Dana Watts's life takes a sudden turn when an unexpected interruption arrives in the form of the most beautiful breasts she has ever seen—stripper Laurel Stanley's. (978-1-60282-014-2)

Heartland by Julie Cannon. When political strategist Rachel Stanton and dude ranch owner Shivley McCoy collide on an empty country road, fate intervenes. (978-1-60282-009-8))

Heart 2 Heart by Julie Cannon. Suffering from a devastating personal loss, Kyle Bain meets Lane Connor, and the chance for happiness suddenly seems possible. (978-1-60282-000-5)

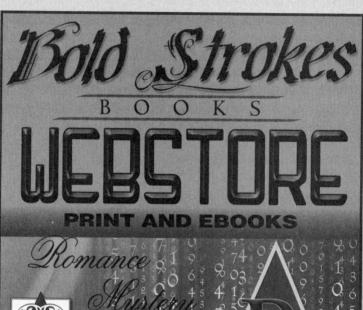